NIAGARA FALLS

100 Years of Souvenirs

NIAGARA FALLS

100 Years of Souvenirs

by

Virginia Vidler

Published by
North Country Books, Inc., Utica, New York

NIAGARA FALLS

100 Years of Souvenirs

by

Virginia Vidler

ISBN Number 0-932052-40-1
Library of Congress Number NK1125.V48
1985   971.3′39   85-8790

Published by
North County Books, Inc., Utica, New York

Contents

Acknowledgments

Writing fans out in many directions, encompassing new places and new faces. For me, a book could never be a solitary act, since I depend on the expertise and good natures of people "in the know."

Three such people have been of continuous help in this three year project: Donald E. Loker, City Historian at Niagara Falls, New York and Director of the Local History Department of the Public Library there, came up with answers that nobody else could find. He gave us access to his archives as well as the Marjorie Williams Collection of Niagara Falls souvenirs housed there.

Charles H. Boyer, retired Director of the Niagara County Historical Society, Lockport, N.Y., who is a collector and antiques authority, patiently led us through the sequence of pertinent historical data relating to souvenirs.

John Burtniak, of Thorold, Ontario and Librarian at Brock University in St. Catharines, is a foremost authority on Niagara Falls and the Niagara River. Not only was he kind enough to unpack his tremendous collection for my husband to photograph, but he also filled in missing data and helped, along with Mr. Loker and Mr. Boyer, in editing the final manuscript.

Through the afore-mentioned gentlemen, we were led to other collections and sources of information. We appreciate the time and patience given, along with access to the following collections pictured in this book:

Dr. & Mrs. John Prout, Mr. & Mrs. Norman MacAskill, Nancy L. Engle, The Native American Center, Niagara Falls, N.Y., The Maid of the Mist Boat Corp. for allowing us to look through their scrapbooks and photo albums, and to Mr. Burt Rosenberg, Niagara Gift Shop, near the falls on the American side, for access to his personal collection of Potter family spar jewelry.

Thanks also to ever-patient librarians at the Buffalo & Erie County Historical Society, The Albright-Knox Art Gallery, Buffalo, and the Erie County Library.

Original art and prints were viewed at The Niagara Parks Commission, Ontario, Canada, the New York City Public Library, The Frick Art Reference Library, New York City, and The Corcoran Gallery of Art, Washington, D.C.

Finally, there would be no reason for doing these acknowledgments, for there would be no book were it not for the talents and patience of my husband/photographer, Edward Vidler and my friend and copy editor, Beverly F. Stoughton.

To all of you . . . it has been fun, I say thanks, and "I'll be your's till Niagara Falls!"

V.V.

Introduction

Since modern man first saw Niagara Falls, it has been one of the most visited spots on the face of the earth. In 1984, for example, this Seventh Natural Wonder of the World attracted over 12 million people to view its power and beauty. Ask foreigners planning a visit to America or Canada what they would like to see first, and nine out of ten will name Niagara Falls. Inquire of foreign students why they picked the Niagara Frontier as an area in which to attend college, and frequently they will reply, "Because we had learned of the falls of Niagara."

Every day, thousands of people line overlooks near the falls. Mist rising from the swirling rapids sprays into their faces. The roar of the cascading falls is so loud that they have to shout to make themselves heard, and the ground vibrates beneath their feet. The experience of viewing the two-mile panorama of Niagara Falls has always been mesmerizing, prompting people to buy souvenirs.

Souvneirs are impulse items intended to remind owners of a specific place or occasion. They are tiny slices of scenic history affixed to such objects as cups and saucers, jugs, thimbles, jewelry boxes, postcards, and a profusion of other saleable pieces that enterprising manufacturers have created over the years. Probably no scenes from North America have been produced more consistently on pictorial souvenirs than those of Niagara Falls. Looked at in sequence, these souvenirs unveil 150 years of fads and follies in the behavior and imaginations of people; provide glimpses into human nature, and recall significant past events as well as transitions in lifestyles. For example, a silk fringed pillow featuring a scene of the falls and MOTHER emblazoned on its velvet cover was purchased by a World War II Soldier on leave at the falls. Another souvenir, a bone china cup, commemorates Queen Mother Elizabeth's visit to the falls in 1939 and occupies a place of high honor in a china cabinet.

Since they were made to appeal to a wide spectrum of society known as tourists, some souvenirs were designed artistically, others gaudily. Likewise, they ranged in prices from a nickel to fifty dollars. Pre-World War II souvenirs were manufactured in England, Austria, Bavaria, Czechoslovakia, Germany, Japan, Canada, and the United States.

1985 will require a new commemorative souvenir, one that celebrates 100 years since the opening of the beautiful parks surrounding Niagara Falls on both sides of the river. Today, tourists cross the Niagara River on international bridges joining Canada and the United States and are free to enjoy the scenic parks and overlooks along both sides. But these parks evolved gradually and not without conflicts of interests regarding the development of industry versus tourism in the Niagara Falls area.

Actually, Niagara Falls is a plural word referring to three falls; the American and Luna (also called the Bridal Veil) Falls that are within the United States, and the Canadian Horseshoe Falls, through whose center the International Boundary runs. Straddling the border between the United States and Canada, Niagara Falls is one of the few natural wonders that is easily accessible by car or foot.

The falls are located on the Niagara River, which connects two great bodies of water, Lakes Erie and Ontario. Water from four other Great Lakes — Superior, Michigan, Huron, and Erie — is carried by the Niagara River into Lake Ontario. This fast moving river is 36 miles long and drops 326 feet between Lakes Erie and Ontario. Most of this drop is over the escarpment at the falls. Although not the tallest falls in the world, Niagara Falls has the greatest volume of water going over it. In its original state, the force of the water flow had energy equal to the power of six million horses! Today, this flow is controlled by a U.S.-Canadian Treaty worked out as a compromise to ensure water power for two conflicting interests — industry and tourism — vital to both countries.

A series of intake gates above the falls allow 350,000 gallons per second to flow over the brink from October to April of each year. On April 1, the flow is doubled, increasing the white-water rapids above the falls and raising the river by 11 feet. In the evening, the flow is cut to half the daytime flow for industrial use; but tourists are not aware of the change because the remaining volume of water is still tremendous and spectacular.

The history of the falls at Niagara is more than famous cascading waters, more than visits of royalty and building landmarks; it is also a parade of tourists from all over the world and the social history reflected in the souvenirs they purchased.

CHAPTER 1

Setting the Scene

Souvenirs of Niagara Falls offer a testimonial to man's imagination and daring set against the background of a spectacular scenic wonder. It may seem unnecessary to separate the American and Canadian Falls in terms of art work used on souvenirs; but the scenes on objects did vary. Such details as changing geography, demolished landmarks and bridges date souvenirs, making one common, another rare.

Artists, standing on one spot, had an entire panorama of Niagara Falls from which to select points of view. Many souvenir scenes were labeled simply *Niagara Falls*, *From Niagara Falls*, or *Souvenir of Niagara Falls* because such titles made items saleable on either side of the border and did not pin down manufacturers to specific historic details. But landmarks such as Cataract House, Cantilever Bridge, Suspension Bridge, or Terrapin Tower, often included in souvenir art, reveal the period in time during which the scenes were created.

The First Tourists

Long before white explorers ventured up the Niagara River to see the falls, they had heard the Indians of the area describe them in Seneca language and gestures as "a place where the river falls from a rock higher than the tallest pines." The Indians had no written language, and French explorers did not speak the Seneca dialect. Based on the sound of the word they heard, they wrote down *Onguiaahra*. A hundred years and twenty-one spellings later, the name evolved as Niagara, supposedly the Indians' term for "the thunderer of waters." In reality, it meant "neck", a connecting waterway (the Niagara River) between the two lakes.

Awesome as they were, the thundering falls were not of great importance to the Indians of the area. Their interest centered on the river crossing near Lewiston because they knew better than to attempt the rapids near the falls in their birchbark canoes.

The first written description of the falls was set down in 1678 by Father Hennepin, a French priest. The area was then known as part of the New World and it was believed that the Niagara River held the key to an all-water route from the St. Lawrence River in Canada to the upper Great Lakes and inland America toward the Mississippi and on to Mexico. It was also believed that whatever country claimed ownership to the land surrounding the waterways would have access to unlimited furs and precious natural resources. French ships had sailed the Niagara River, entering from Lake Ontario at a point where old Fort Niagara now stands. They sailed up the river against a strong current, but only to within hearing distance of the roaring falls. From the local inhabitants, the Seneca Indians of the Iroquois Nation, the explorers learned of *Onguiaahra*, a falls so high that they claimed it stunned even the fish; and they recorded "some sort of an Indian carrying place or a portage around the falls," where the Indians scaled the river banks 165 feet high loaded down with goods on their backs.

One of the most famous and daring of the North American explorers, Robert Cavelier, Sieur de la Salle, determined to be the first to make a voyage to the upper lakes to trade for furs. In 1678, he sent a scouting party that included Father Hennepin into Indian country to make contact with the Senecas. It was LaSalle's plan to sail into the Niagara River below the falls with a ship loaded with materials, carpenters, and blacksmiths for building another ship above the falls.

By plying them with rum and tobacco, LaSalle's scouting party persuaded the Indians to lead them over their "carrying place" through the forest and along the high banks of the river around the falls. Six tons of supplies and five dismantled cannons were carried ten miles. The project, begun in December of 1678, was completed in August of 1679. LaSalle's newly built ship, the *Griffon*, entered Lake Erie — the first ship ever to do so. White men had pushed further into the Indians' lands, deceptively calling their fortifications storehouses or castles, in order to allay the Indians' suspicions.

Father Hennepin kept detailed journals of the LaSalle expedition and drew the first known sketch of the falls. This sketch, though bearing little resemblance to the falls as seen today, has been continuously reproduced in texts and prints.

The *Griffon's* voyage into Lake Erie began the struggle for control of the area. For more than a hundred years after LaSalle's mission, Niagara was the constant scene of battles, skirmishes and the building of fortifications. French, British, Iroquois Indians, and American colonists fought for control of the Niagara region and the wilderness surrounding it. Furs were the lucrative reward for the victors.

By the time of the American Revolution, Fort Niagara had become the center for Indian trade and any social life that developed in the Niagara region during the Colonial period. Indian foot trails through the forest gradually developed into rutted dirt roads wide enough at first for wagons and later, for stage coaches. Saw and grist mills were built to harness the first power taken from the Niagara River. Ships from Europe brought cloth, brass, cast-iron household wares, Indian trade goods, and munitions to Fort Niagara. The first railway on the North American continent was built by the British at the present site of Lewiston. It was an ingenious tramway up the face of the escarpment. Two cars attached to ropes connected with a drum ran up and down wood piers with goods from arriving ships. The tramway, along with wagon roads built along the portage route, conveyed tons of supplies. It also put the Indians out of work portering the goods on foot.

The final hostilities in the Niagara region took place during the War of 1812, fought by Britain and America. Since that time, Canada and the United States have enjoyed peaceful relationships, friendly borders, and shared ownership of the falls.

Power from Niagara

The building of the Welland and Erie Canals in the mid-1800's provided the solution to the problem of getting around the falls. Men now turned from portages to power. They were inspired, not with the grandeur of the falls, but with the 70 million gallons of water per minute rushing over the crest. It offered potential energy if it could be harnessed.

In 1877, after others had tried unsuccessfully, Jacob F. Schoellkopf first extracted power from the Niagara River to operate his flour mills. Towards the 1890's Niagara became the home of many of the brilliant pioneers of today's electro-chemistry and electro-metallurgy industries. Their products included aluminum; calcium carbide that resulted in the replacement of kerosene lamps with clear acetylene gas; carborundum, a new grinding material; and artificial graphite used for industrial purposes.

One of the best known industries resulting from Niagara's electric power was the Shredded Wheat Company. For years, the ornate yellow-brick factory was an attraction second only to the falls. White-suited guides conducted tourists through the factory where they saw an amazing electrically-operated conveyor belt on which lay hundreds of golden biscuits. The factory was a new concept in 1901 and the tours made this natural food a best seller. Niagara Falls became nationally known as "The Home of Shredded Wheat."

Industries, large and small, began to line both sides of the Niagara River near the falls where there was electricity. Fortunes were made — and lost — on speculation. The Niagara region boomed with employment and commerce, but it also moved toward an inevitable clash of interests. Many of those not involved with power from the river grasped the opportunity to capitalize on the view.

Tourism Takes Over

As early as 1829, the first guidebook ever published about Niagara Falls estimated that 35 to 50 thousand people, "the fashionable, the opulent, and the learned," would visit there as part of the *Grand Tours* of the east. These affluent people, touring cities along the Hudson River in private horsedrawn coaches, continued west to the falls area.

But the real influx of tourists began in the 1850's when a railroad system was put into operation. Passengers, wearing dusters to protect themselves from soot and sparks, boarded trains every half hour to ride along the top of the gorge overlooking the falls. There was a special line bringing passengers from the Erie Canal in Lockport and excursion trains from Buffalo, New York and Philadelphia. Tourists poured into many hotels, inns, restaurants, and souvenir shops that clustered near the falls. Boarding houses and gambling saloons sprang up everywhere.

Not surprisingly, the magnificent natural wonder was obscured by a barrage of promotional schemes and outlandish activities that went on around the falls. A guidebook warned:

"Much has been said about the hackmen at Niagara. These much abused individuals are noted for their perseverence, and the zeal which they manifest in their business and their ignorance of the word, 'no'."

Hackmen weren't the only problem. Hawkers shouted on every corner. For a fee, guides offered to escort tourists down the treacherous gorge on foot trails to the base of the falls, and then collected an extra fee to lead them back up. Toll booths mushroomed, charging fees for access to areas along the overlooks, walled from view by high board fences.

Eventually, the entire area took on a carnival atmosphere. People who lived in the two cities of Niagara Falls could barely move out of their yards, let alone enjoy the scenic wonder. Daredevils performed stunts over the falls in hopes of instant wealth and fame as thousands of spectators lined the banks, cheering them on.

During this same period, technology had advanced to the point where industry, if allowed, could have diverted for its own use most of the flow of water from the falls, thereby destroying the phenomena.

In 1885, the two governments, pressured by the public, acquired ownership of their respective falls and surrounding acreage. Slowly, the area was developed into the park systems that exist today for the enjoyment of all.

Each souvenir is a tiny slice of this rich and varied history. Activities centering around Niagara Falls have involved the coming and going of horsedrawn coaches, steam locomotives, many *Maid of the Mist* boats, assorted grand hotels, and a volume of mementos. In the midst of all this change, the water cascading over the falls appears the same. Actually, the rate of its flow is controlled and the escarpment over which it runs is ever-changing, slowly shifting and eroding with time.

One can determine where souvenirs fit into the past history of the falls. A fine oil painting by an artist of the Hudson River School of Painting or a Staffordshire platter dating to the early 1800's, are pieces from the elegant period. A beautifully beaded 1890 pin cushion from the Tuscarora Reservation near the falls tells of the Indians' involvement in the souvenir trade, while a risque little peep show exposing ladies' ankles reflects the bawdy era in falls history. Railroad excursion posters, stock certificates, timetables, and advertisements such as *Niagara Falls, Home of Shredded Wheat*, represent only a few souvenirs from the commercial enterprises of an area that grew to be the greatest natural tourist attraction on earth.

Pag. 24. Part y 1.st

Father Hennepin's sketch, the first one done in 1678.
Courtesy of: Local History Dept., Niagara Falls, N.Y. Public Library.

Power from Niagara. Scene from the Jacob Schoellkopf files showing development of the lower milling district, c 1900.
Courtesy of: Local History Dept., Niagara Falls, N.Y. Public Library.

Postcard scenes of power plants along both sides of the Niagara River near the falls.
Courtesy of: Local History Dept., Niagara Falls, N.Y. Public Library.

The Shredded Wheat factory, a marvel to tourists in its day.

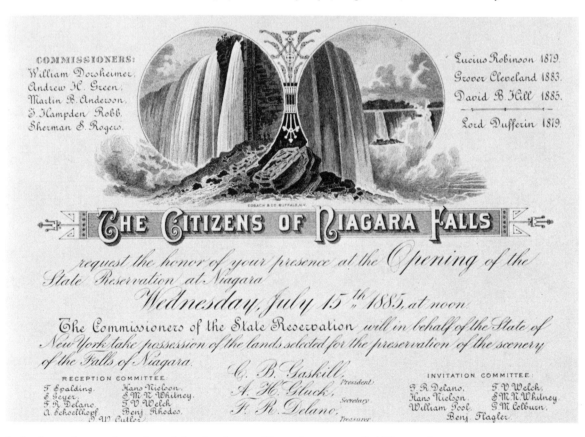

Invitation to the grand opening celebration for a public park system, called Niagara Reservation, New York State's first State Park. 1885.

Tourists setting out to enjoy "the wonders of Niagara" in a horse-drawn wagon. Early 1900's.
Courtesy of Niagara County Historical Society, Inc., Lockport, N.Y.

The Giant Rock, Great Gorge Route, Niagara Falls

The Great Gorge Route conveyed tourists in steel trolley cars.
Courtesy of: Niagara County Historical Society, Inc., Lockport, N.Y.

CHAPTER 2

Scenes on Souvenirs

Most souvenirs depict views that were popular and current during the time of manufacture because they were intended to help people remember what they had actually seen on their visits to the falls.

Scenes on early souvenirs were taken from artists' works. After the advent of photography and pictorial postcards, photo illustrations were commonly used on souvenirs. Thus, background details such as buildings, towers, and bridges can be useful in pinpointing the period in which a souvenir was issued.

Shapes of souvenirs and the materials from which they were made are also clues to dating objects. Earlier ones tended to be small, reflecting the mode of travel. They were made to fit into handbags or pockets. Shot glasses, miniature top hats, small pitchers, compact guide books, and six-inch plates were examples. Materials such as milk glass, depression glass, or aluminum also date objects.

Any or all or these details — scenes, shapes or materials of manufacture — are tip-offs that help verify the age of souvenirs.

Following are the titles and descriptions of those scenes that were most frequently used on souvenirs. The 1882 Niagara Falls, New York, aerial view and photo illustrations copied from 1884 and 1892 guide books for use in this chapter are also examples of photography — a category in itself, covered in the last chapter.

BOTH FALLS FROM ABOVE: Looking down on the two falls from high on the Canadian escarpment in 1882, one could see the upper Suspension Bridge (wooden towers), the American Falls and, the smaller Luna Falls (also known as The Bridal Veil Falls), Goat Island and the Canadian Horseshoe Falls. Overall views such as this one were popular for paintings and photographs, but included too much detail to be reduced on objects such as plates or cups.

GENERAL VIEW OF THE FALLS FROM CANADA: This is the most common title found on souvenirs of the past, as well as the present. Only the surrounding landmarks have changed! One vantage point was from high above, on the site of the Loretto Convent, still standing today. Another was from a spot called Inspiration Point, near the present Rainbow Bridge. For several centuries, artists have lingered at this easily accessible spot to absorb the panorama and sound of Niagara while attempting to capture its mightiness on canvas or film. Artists were free to embellish their works with shoreline greenery or branches that added perspective and a third dimension to the view. Viewed from the Canadian side, a splendid rainbow arches over the Horseshoe Falls when the afternoon sun shines on it. This famous rainbow, for which the bridge was named, is a spectacular feature often emphasized on souvenirs. *General View* lent itself to large, horizontal formats — oil paintings, platters, serving trays — also to small rectangular shapes such as paperweights and postcards.

HORSESHOE FALLS: The Canadian Horseshoe Falls, named after its shape, is wider than the American Falls. Ten times more water flows over it. Because of its unique shape, the immense volume of water going over it, and the often visible rainbow, *Horseshoe Falls* is probably the second most popular scene used on souvenirs. The original horseshoe appearance is slowly eroding away due to more water going over the center and less over the sides. Water hitting the rocks at the base of the falls also causes the ever-present mist that fills the air. The rainbow, said to be the only one in the world that forms a perfect circle, can be seen on any sunny day. In winter, the mist crystalizes, resulting in dramatic ice formations. *Horseshoe Falls*, also called *Rainbow Falls*, appears on souvenirs from a variety of vantage points. The scenes on souvenirs were labeled "Horseshoe (or Rainbow) Falls From": *Canada, The American Side, Prospect Point, Table Rock, Goat Island*, and *General View of Horseshoe Falls*. Boulders at the base of the falls and a steam-powered Maid of the Mist boat were frequently included in Horseshoe Falls scenes. The boats are now diesel powered. The vertical format of this view adapted nicely to such objects as silver spoon handles, small plates, glass tumblers, playing cards, and glass transparencies.

AMERICAN FALLS: Although not as wide or uniquely shaped as the Horseshoe Falls, the geography around the American Falls side of the river offers a variety of dramatic points of interest from which the falls can be seen. A general view of the falls is titled, *American Falls from Canada*. It includes the Cataract House and International Hotel on the horizon line. Other views, used on a huge assortment of souvenirs, are titled, "American Falls From": *Prospect Point, Goat Island, Three Sisters Islands, Cave of the Winds, The Rapids, Whirlpool*, and *Winter Scene*.

PROSPECT POINT: As a scene, Prospect Point rivaled the American and Horseshoe Falls in popularity. Almost directly opposite the vantage point in Canada for the General View of the two falls, Prospect Point is at the northern-most edge of land near the American Falls. It is as close to the brink of the falls as one can stand. From this spot, artists could see and select views from a mile-long span of the Niagara crestline. They also ventured down 300 steep stone steps (before the advent of elevators) to the gorge below in order to do scenes labeled *Below Prospect Point*. Art work done from Prospect Point usually included the edge of the point in the foreground and both falls in the background. The scene adapted well to round souvenirs such as plates, paperweights, dress pins and compacts.

GOAT ISLAND: This is an unglamorous name for 70 acres of land considered to be one of the outstanding natural sanctuaries in the United States. Decades ago, it was a mecca for artists and naturalists because of the variety of undisturbed plant, animal, and bird life. The name derives from a story about a farmer who, in the autumn of 1765, put his animals on the island for the winter to protect them from wolves. The harsh weather proved too much for all but one goat who survived till spring and had a scenic wonder named in his honor. At one time, it was suggested that the name be officially changed to Iris Island in order to more closely identify with the area's floral beauty, but the name Goat Island prevailed. Today, although well-trampled by millions of tourists over the years, it is still a beautiful park with overlooks from which to experience, at the closest range possible, the two falls and whirlpool rapids directly below.

Other titles of scenes on souvenirs include: *Bath Island, Luna Island, Terrapin Rocks, Terrapin Tower, Table Rock, Whirlpool Rapids, Bridal Veil Falls, Rock of Ages*, and *Biddle Stairs*.

1882 Map showing L-R: The American Falls; the small Luna (also called Bridal Veil Falls); Goat Island; The Canadian Horseshoe Falls; Table Rock jutting out at bottom center of photo; and a carriage roadway from Table Rock to the famous Clifton House in Canada. Bridge is the Upper Suspension Bridge.

Horseshoe Falls scenes, taken from the Canadian side, usually include a Maid of the Mist boat steaming through the water. From an 1892 guide book.

Looking directly at the American Falls from the Canadian side, Cataract House and International Hotel appear on the horizon line and the railing of the walkway to Rock of Ages and Cave of the Winds are below. Taken from an 1892 guide book.

Both Falls from Prospect Point is most commonly pictured on souvenirs. Taken from an 1892 guide book.

View of the falls taken from the Convent, Canadian side. Street's Pagoda, an observation tower, shows on the right.

Rock of Ages and Cave of the Winds, another popular view was frequently adapted to souvenirs. Taken from an 1884 guide book.

Horseshoe Falls from below, Canadian Side. Taken from an 1884 souvenir guide book.

The Horseshoe Falls from below Table Rock was a spectacular view and the subject of a great assortment of art work, often featuring people in rain slickers. Taken from an 1884 guide book.

CHAPTER 3

Landmarks and Bridges

Historic preservationists could find a wealth of reference material on pictorial souvenirs. Landmarks and bridges included in scenes add details for discovering the year of issue or period from which the on-the-scene art work was taken. It is worth repeating the fact that souvenirs usually bore current scenes that tourists had just visited and that most scenes were copied from photographed views.

Referring to the 1882 aerial view of Niagara Falls, N.Y. in Chapter 2, it can be seen that the American Falls has a horizon line in its background while the Canadian Horseshoe Falls does not. Any souvenir scene labeled with the general title, *Niagara Falls* can thereby be identified as either the American or Horseshoe Falls.

Two roof lines appear frequently in scenes of the American Falls. They are those of the Cataract House and International Hotel. These buildings spanned the years 1853 - 1918, when they stood next to each other on the river's edge, just above the falls. Wooden bridges led to Goat Island, where tourists could then walk to Terrapin Tower on the further side of Goat Island, next to Horseshoe Falls. Terrapin Tower was named after the terrapin-turtle-shaped rocks below it. The tower was also called *Horseshoe* or *Prospect Tower*. Built in 1833, the stone tower was 43 feet high, 12 feet in diameter at the base and 8 feet at the top where there was a gallery. The tower was destroyed in 1873, supposedly because it was hazardous but more likely (according to old texts) because it drew tourists and their cash away from concessions at Prospect Point. Rivalry was fierce before the area became a public park system.

Terrapin Tower offered a challenging and spectacular view for the adventuresome while Clifton House, on the Canadian side, was a luxurious vantage point. Although Clifton House is not pictured on souvenirs, many were titled *View from Clifton House*. This elegant hotel offered the ultimate view of both falls. It was here that the aristocratic classes from the South were often accommodated preceding the Civil War. The original Clifton House was built in 1833 and burned down in 1895. It was replaced with a far more elegant Clifton House which remained in business until another fire destroyed it in 1932. The present Sheraton Brock Hotel occupies the site.

Cataract House, International Hotel, and Clifton House were by no means the only hotels that served the immediate falls area. It was ringed with lesser known hotels and tourist inns. However, souvenirs, pictures, announcements, advertisements or other memorabilia from less famous hotels were quite unlikely to be found.

Table Rock projected over the escarpment. It was within leisurely strolling distance or carriage drive from Clifton House. Because of its vantage point, Table Rock was as important to artists as Goat Island to naturalists. Scenes taken from Table Rock were very popular and common on souvenirs. These scenes can be dated because there were frequent rock slides at Table Rock, which remained a favorite vantage point until 1850. At that time, a piece of Table Rock 200 feet long and 60 feet wide fell into the gorge below. The thundering repercussion was heard for miles in all directions. Table Rock remained a vantage point of much less spectacular proportions until 1930 when the remaining ledge was blasted away in the name of public safety, destroying the site forever.

Gone are the days of the grand old hotels, slippery narrow pathways to the river's edge and "at your own risk" access to dangerous overlooks such as Terrapin Tower. Fires, demolitions, nature, progress, and public liability requirements have done away with most of them, leaving only souvenir scenes as valuable remembrances.

Bridges

Engineering and railroad history was made at Niagara Falls where the world's first and longest bridges were built across the Niagara River, linking Canada and the United States for the first time.

Early bridges were hung from wooden supports (pylons) on each bank, which is why they were called suspension bridges. They swayed with heavy traffic and winds. The next engineering development, the cantilever type bridge, consisted of trusses built on each side of the river bank. They projected toward each other and were joined in the middle. Further advances made possible the construction of strong steel bridges that arched over the river — therefore the name steel arch bridges. All three of these bridge designs — suspension, cantilever, and steel arch — will be noted on souvenirs.

It is intriguing that over a hundred years of world-famous bridge building achievements at Niagara Falls began with a kite flying contest! But in 1848, Charles Ellet, who had received a contract to build the first bridge across the river, found it necessary to get a line over the 800-foot gorge before he began the job. He came up with the idea of a kite flying contest and advertised a $5 reward for any boy who could get his kite from one side of the river to the other. Contestants crowded opposite banks of the river near the construction site. On the second day of the contest, a boy on the American side landed his kite in Canada. The kite string was tied to a tree, a light cord attached to the end and painstakingly pulled across the chasm. Next, a heavier cord was attached to the light one and it was pulled over, followed by a rope, a wire, and finally a heavy cable that spanned the river to begin construction of the first suspension bridge. The wooden-floored bridge was built for foot and carriage traffic. Until then, the only means of transportation for tourists between the Canadian and American sides was by rowboat.

The first suspension bridge was a very successful venture, but it wasn't long before the idea of building a bridge with the capacity for both carriages and trains came up. In 1855, a second suspension bridge was built to replace the first one. As a matter of fact, the first bridge was used as a scaffolding to erect the second; and then it was dismantled.

At the time, it seemed impossible that trains could go over a suspension bridge. But John A. Roebling, who later engineered the Brooklyn Bridge, designed the world's first such bridge at Niagara Falls. It was hailed as, "one of the grandest triumphs of human skill on the globe." Hung from wire cables that were 230 feet above the Whirlpool Rapids, the *Suspension Bridge* became as big an attraction as the falls. It had two levels, the upper one for trains, and the lower for horse-drawn vehicles. Roebling was so confident of his design that he rode with the engineer on the first 368-ton train to cross the bridge. Over the years, the bridge had to be re-engineered to support heavier trains and the demands of increased traffic.

Because it was a first and of worldwide fame, *The Railway Suspension Bridge* was pictured on many items such as commemorative prints for framing, postcards, railroad company ads, slingers, and tickets. The name Suspension Bridge became synonymous with Niagara Falls. Passengers were thrilled to go to "The Big Bridge," as it was called, and marvelled at riding over it. Illustrations of the bridge that Roebling designed clearly show two levels or decks with a train on the upper one. It is distinguished from earlier suspension bridges by the two decks. Artists were able to create the illusion, for the purposes of railroad advertisements, of this bridge being very close to the falls. But it wasn't. The falls were two miles distant because the early bridges had to be built at the narrowest point on the river, near the Whirlpool Rapids. Later, engineering technology made it possible to span a wider section of the river, closer to the falls, which is why a bridge near the falls was the next logical development in the competition for tourists.

Instead of a kite flying contest, the 1868 winter ice jam was used to walk the first cable across the river in order to begin constructing a suspension bridge for carriages that was within close view of both falls. Currier & Ives published a print of this *Falls View Bridge* for release in 1868. With two bridges on the scene, they logically became known by locations: *Lower bridges* were those built lower on the river where Roebling's railway suspension was erected. Later ones, closer to the falls, were further up the river and therefore became known as *Upper* or *Falls View Bridges*. To further complicate the subject, each time bridges were re-engineered, names were changed! But these changes are helpful in dating souvenirs.

Amazingly, traffic never halted during 15 complete reconstruction projects as bridges were revamped to meet changing traffic weights and patterns from horse-drawn carriages to trains to automobiles. The work went over, under, around, and next to existing structures while tourists continued to pour into the falls area.

Today, there are three bridges linking the U.S. and Canada: The Rainbow Bridge near the falls where the first Upper or Falls View bridges were located; a Canadian National Railroad bridge where Roebling's first Suspension Bridge was erected (about two miles down river from the Rainbow Bridge); and a bridge at Lewiston, in the vicinity of Fort Niagara.

Cataract House stood next to the International Hotel. Built in 1814, it was destroyed by a fire in 1945.

Courtesy of: Local History Dept., Niagara Falls, N.Y. Public Library.

- THE INTERNATIONAL HOTEL -

THE NEAREST HOTEL TO THE FALLS. ○ THE LARGEST HOTEL AT NIAGARA.
THE MOST MODERN AND THE BEST IN ALL ITS APPOINTMENTS.

THE Hotel will open on the 1st of June, and will continue open until late in October. Over $40,000 expended in remodelling in 1890. The finest dining room in America The latest sanitary plumbing throughout.

THE management of the Hotel has been entrusted to MR. HORACE FOX, so long and favorably known to the patrons of the Chautauqua Lake resorts.

Magnificent Views of the Islands and Falls from its Piazzas and Dining Room.

SPECIAL RATES FOR FAMILIES.

Write for terms.

One of the Finest Lawns in the World.

INTERNATIONAL HOTEL CO.,
NIAGARA FALLS, N. Y.

RATES, $3 TO $5 PER DAY.

Advertisement for the International Hotel, on the American Side. Built in 1853, destroyed by fire in 1918.

Courtesy of: Local History Dept., Niagara Falls, N.Y. Public Library.

Clifton House, on the Canadian side, was built in 1833 and enlarged over the years before a fire destroyed it in 1898. A second, larger Clifton House built in 1905 to replace this one, was also destroyed by fire in 1932.

Courtesy of: Local History Dept., Niagara Falls, N.Y. Public Library.

This lithograph taken from an 1852 painting by a famous French artist, Hippolyte Sebron, is titled "Scene from Table Rock." It shows the first 'Maid of the Mist' boat built to convey a carriage with a team of horses. Terrapin Tower is seen directly above the boat, on the American side.

Courtesy of: The Maid of the Mist Boat Corp., Niagara Falls, N.Y.

Terrapin Tower stood 45 feet above the water and was considered the most exciting vantage point from which to view the falls. It stood from 1833 to 1873.

Courtesy of: Local History Dept., Niagara Falls, N.Y. Public Library.

Roebling's 1855 'Railway Suspension Bridge', built with two decks, the upper for trains, and the lower for horse-drawn vehicles.

Courtesy of: Local History Dept., Niagara Falls, N.Y. Public Library.

The 'Railway Suspension Bridge' was considered one of man's greatest engineering triumphs when it was built in 1855. It was greatly publicized by railroad companies.

Courtesy of: Niagara County Historical Society, Inc., Lockport, N.Y.

The Cantilever and Suspension Railway Bridges were within a few hundred yards of each other, spanning the gorge above the Whirlpool Rapids. They were known as "Lower Bridges".

The 'Railway Suspension Bridge' was eventually replaced with a Steel Arch Bridge in 1898. Behind it, the Cantilever Bridge can be seen.

Courtesy of: Local History Dept., Niagara Falls, N.Y. Public Library.

The 'Steel Arch Bridge' was also known as the Honeymoon Bridge. It appears frequently on souvenir scenes, which dates them to pre-1938 when the bridge collapsed.
Courtesy of: Local History Dept., Niagara Falls, N.Y. Public Library.

CHAPTER 4

China and Glass

Historically, china and glass have been the most popular of all the Niagara Falls collectible items. Women have always been partial to buying cups and saucers, serving platters, bowls, candy dishes, vases and knickknacks. Also, Niagara Falls is known as "The Honeymoon Capital of the World," attracting thousands of newlyweds eager to purchase such remembrances for their new homes.

To meet this great sales potential, Niagara Falls shops imported china from England, France, Ireland, Austria, Bavaria, Germany, and Japan. Plates, platters, and cups and saucers were the best sellers, followed by mugs, vases, pitchers, food-serving trays, dresser trays, teapots, tumblers, and novelties such as top hats, slippers and hearts. Shaving mugs, matched sets of salts and peppers, and water pitchers are somewhat scarce as collectible finds today — probably because people tended to use them more than the other objects, which were often stored away to use on special occasions or when company came.

China

Although usually called by the generic name china, these souvenirs range in type and quality from utilitarian pottery to fine porcelain. They span nearly 125 years of changing lifestyles and represent the largest assortment of all the Niagara Falls souvenirs.

A variety of serving dishes were manufactured for table use during the Victorian Period from the mid-to-late 1800's, when niceties were observed in the extreme. Household help was easily and inexpensively obtained. Consider the fact that as many as a hundred pieces of dinnerware often were set for a formal at-home meal, and one can begin to appreciate the variety of china once available to homemakers. Underliners, salt dips, nappies, compotes, cream pitchers, bone dishes, coasters, meat platters and custard dishes are but a few of the items from this period that appeared as souvenirs of Niagara Falls.

Niagara Falls was used as a motif on fine china items not intended for tourist shops at the falls, but for marketing with other American scenic pieces in great demand at the turn of the century. Commemorative and historic plates were very popular, having been introduced for the Centennial of 1876 held in Philadelphia. It became fashionable to have American scenes on display throughout the home. Plates were hung on walls and placed on plate rails. Scenes from Niagara Falls were particularly desirable and in vogue during this era.

Considering the quantities and varieties of china that were produced, it is surprising that no complete sets of Niagara Falls dinnerware were marketed. A person may have purchased four, six, or eight of the same dessert plates or cups and saucers from a counter, but the items did not originate as matched sets.

Commercial or restaurant grade china, with Niagara Falls imprinted on it, did not originate as souvenirs, but is a great find for collectors today. It was used in hotels, inns,

27

convention halls, and railroad dining cars in the falls area. Such pieces offer two points of history — a scene of the falls, and the name of a business or railroad that once operated there.

Because of the diverse homelands of tourists who originally purchased souvenir china, it is scattered in the four corners of the world. It turns up everywhere. Many pieces show little or no signs of wear, retaining gold-leaf lettering, gilding and art work in original condition.

Were the scenes used on souvenirs from Niagara Falls authentic? An expert says:

"There was so much Niagara Falls art work done and available for reproduction that most of the scenes were from original, on-the-spot artists' renderings. Once in a while, you'll find a piece of pre-World War II Japan with a falls scene that is obviously just any falls labelled Niagara. But transfer printing was the common process used on early souvenirs. Photographs were reproduced on later ones."

The process of transfer printing is exactly what the name implies; an original engraving done on a copper plate using special ink and a sheet of thin but strong paper to pick up the picture. While still wet, the paper is pressed on the china piece, thereby transferring the art work to the object. The finishing work — coloring or painting, firing and glazing — is done last. This process, invented in the mid-1700's, first made it possible for people of average means to afford beautifully decorated dishes.

Canadians and Colonial Americans who emigrated from England were naturally partial to tableware imported from the mother country rather than from other countries in Europe. As a result, the china-producing districts of England, known as The Potteries, (Staffordshire, Liverpool, Burslem, Bristol, Leeds and Sunderland) did a flourishing business creating export china that they knew would be popular over here.

One of the most favored was the transfer-printed pottery now called Staffordshire. Though it was made in a variety of colors — pink, mulberry, brown, light blue — it was the deep, rich blue on white that became the favorite, especially that which depicted historic American scenes.

Staffordshire represents the earliest in china souvenirs of Niagara Falls, dating back to the mid-1800's. The War of 1812 had ruined England's large, lucrative china trade to America. Britain's potters were desperate for new ideas that would win back their business. Shrewdly, they decided to put American views on Staffordshire pieces. The idea was an immediate hit. By 1825, more china was coming to America in a month than had come in a full year during the 1790's. For example, a monthly shipment to a single outlet in Philadelphia consisted of 262,000 pieces of Staffordshire! More than 700 views of American scenery, buildings, steamboats, and George Washington were used by over 30 Staffordshire pottery firms in England.

English potters weren't the only ones vying for the American market. Manufacturers in Austria, Germany, and France were mass-producing stock pieces (or blanks) on which to transfer American and Canadian scenes. Among them were various views of Niagara Falls, which was fast becoming a mecca for tourists.

It would be convenient if all the 1825 - 1890 pieces were clearly and completely marked, but manufacturers were inconsistent in regard to which wares and how many items in each lot they marked. It is possible to have two identical Niagara Falls pieces, one marked, and the other not. However, the lack of marks on the backs of Niagara Falls china should not be discouraging, for there are other ways to date it.

Many experts agree that old Staffordshire can be distinguished from new by the presence of stilt or spur marks arranged in a triangular pattern on the backs of china pieces. Many early pieces were small because of the mode of transportation. They had to fit into handbags or pockets.

Earthenware produced by Josiah Wedgwood also came to this country and Canada as Niagara Falls souvenirs. The wares included his famous jasperware in blue, green, gray-green, black, and other colors, decorated with raised white designs of the falls. This pottery is unglazed and the raised decorations create a cameo effect, for which Wedgwood is best known. Most of the items produced were, and still are, display pieces, such as ornate vases, pitchers, bowls and teapots — elegant in their classic and clean designs. Not all jasperware is Wedgwood. As was common in England when a pottery developed a profitable ware, other companies soon discovered the formula and cashed in by producing the same ware or some of lesser quality. Original Wedgwood pieces are impressed with a circular mark and the word "Wedgwood". It is worth noting that another pottery operated under the name Wedgewood, spelled with an "e". It should not be confused with Josiah Wedgwood's output. Jasperware has been made continuously and its popularity has never diminished over the years. Wedgwood, always an innovator, also perfected the technique for adding gold, copper, pink and purple lustres in creating unusual decorative effects on china.

Two other well-known English potters are associated with Niagara Falls souvenirs. Spode, who developed bone china in about 1800, and his successor, Copeland. Bone china, made by the addition of bone ash to clay formulas, is distinguished by characteristics of hardness, whiteness, and translucence.

Spode is still being made. Some very collectible contemporary pieces are available which were made by the Carborundum Company in Niagara Falls between 1973 and 1976. This company brought English potters to the United States and set up a complete mini-Spode factory in their ceramic museum. Commemorative scenes of Niagara Falls, adapted from period prints, were transfer-printed on a 16 piece tea set and seven other limited edition pieces of approximately 250 each. Since they were produced for only a short time, they are very limited, and thus desirable.

Ironstone china, patented in 1813 by Charles Mason, is hard, as the name iron indicates, and opaque. It was mass-produced in England for export to America. After 1851, when Mason's patent expired, other potters picked up the formula and made pieces marked "Ironstone" or "English Ironstone." Ridgeway bought out the Mason firm and Ridgeway Ironstone is often marked, as are Wedgwood and Spode ironstone, all coveted antiques today.

Porcelain seldom bore marks, with the exceptions of decorators' marks or factory numbers, but is distinguishable from pottery by its thinness and translucence.

In 1891, the United States Government passed the McKinley Act which required all imports to be marked with the name of the country of origin. The logical conclusion, then, is that any unmarked Niagara Falls piece is at least 80 years old. Wrong! An antiques dealer reminds us that many imports were marked with glued-on paper labels, which, in nearly every case, have disappeared.

Japanese-made souvenirs flooded the Niagara Falls market after World War II. Earlier pieces had the name Nippon or Japan painted on them before firing, or again, they were sometimes marked with paper labels.

"If you were to line up blank pieces of English and Japanese china, they would feel and look alike," commented the dealer, "but there's something different looking about the pieces when they are converted to Japanese souvenirs," she continued. "It's the quality of the art work that differs — blurriness of the transferred prints and colors used on their souvenirs."

It was interesting to learn how and where people came by the souvenirs pictured in this chapter. Although the very fine and rare pieces had been acquired by owners who had always collected quality anitques, not just Niagara Falls souvenirs, others had obtained theirs within the last five or ten years.

One collector, who only recently began shopping household sales, flea markets, and small shows, has accumulated many Niagara Falls pieces — including unmarked, old Spode and jasperware at giveaway prices.

Naturally, breakage has taken a toll over the years. Today, a buyer must often abandon selectivity in favor of any piece of china depicting Niagara Falls. Sometimes the bad comes with the good - cups without saucers, saucers without cups, biscuit jars, tureens and compotes without lids. People readily adapt such pieces, enjoying them as planters, ash trays, and gift containers for homemade jelly or candy. And there is always the lure and possibility of finding an early Staffordshire plate or six identical fruit dishes in mint condition that some long-ago bride stored away as precious keepsakes and never used!

Glass

With the exception of some fine pieces made for department and jewelry store trade, glass souvenirs of Niagara Falls were manufactured with inexpensive materials. They were mass-produced, reproductions of old cut glass patterns and the original very expensive blown ruby glass pieces.

Much of the souvenir ruby glass was manufactured in Pittsburgh at the turn of the century. Ruby coloring was added by a method of flashing, staining, or painting all or part of a piece with red. The words "Souvenir Of" were blocked or etched on a souvenir piece, leaving a space for the name of the locality. Pressed glass patterns were generally used on these red pieces, buttons and arches being the most common motifs. Perhaps the use of the old pressed patterns — themselves originally imitations of cut glass patterns — cause this glass to be mistaken for more valuable cut glass. But in its day, ruby-colored and pressed glass was very inexpensive. Today, of course, the prices that these souvenirs bring as collectibles would astound the original buyers.

Milk glass was another popular and inexpensive variety of glass used to make souvenir plates in the 1920's and 30's. Depression glass in a variety of colors - green, yellow, pink, blue, orange - was also used for souvenirs in this period.

Glass paperweights are almost a separate and very popular collecting category today. They offer vignettes of natural history as well as business and promotional activities of the past. Paperweights were also mass produced for souvenir shops. Salesmen called on shop owners with samples of various sizes, shapes and glass quality from which selections were made. Niagara Falls postcard or photo scenes were also selected by shop owners to be factory reduced and glued, facing up, in the bottoms of paperweights. Often, the backing on paperweights will bear the name of a distributor or Niagara Falls merchant. Postcard publishers were frequently also in the paperweight wholesaling business because the two lines were very compatible. Today, collectors acquire and pay for paperweights according to the quality and weight of glass, uncommon shapes, but mainly the uniqueness of scenes. There seems to be a steady demand for Niagara Falls paperweights.

Unlike china, glass souvenirs usually bear no markings to tell where they originated. Occasionally, "RS Prussia" or MS Austria" may appear on the bottom of better pieces.

Although produced in great quantities in German and English factories, only the details in workmanship and scenes on pieces are clues to origins and years.

German souvenirs were usually made of porcelain, hand tinted, and frequently the body had shadings of blue or green added to it. In contrast, British wares were generally transfer-printed in one color.

China and glass souvenirs have always been the largest lines of merchandise in souvenir shops. Most of them were decorative pieces, purchased as treasured reminders of visits to Niagara Falls or for gifts to others. Like most keepsakes, many of these early pieces remained in gift boxes or on knickknack shelves for many, many years. Happily, they turn up today in mint condition.

Staffordshire platter, 15" x 11½", in dark blue. One of the Niagara pieces made for export from England after the War of 1812. Titled "Niagara from The American Side", it is marked Enoch Wood & Sons, Burslem.
     Courtesy of: Niagara County Historical Society, Inc., Lockport, N.Y.

Staffordshire platter by William Adams & Sons, Stoke, England. A rare pink color with a view from Table Rock. This c 1835, 20-inch platter is considered a fine antique today.

Staffordshire pieces which were common export items included this ten-inch dinner plate, dark blue, with Enoch Wood's distinguishing shell and seaweed border and a scene from below Table Rock. c 1820. Next to it, a four-inch beaker imported by The Marsellus Company, a firm in New York City that sold to souvenir shops. c 1900.
Courtesy of: Niagara County Historical Society, Inc., Lockport, N.Y.

View from Prospect point, with The Convent appearing on the horizon line. Applied to an eight-inch plate with orange, iridescent finish. Made in Bavaria. c 1900.
Courtesy of: Nancy Engle.

Prospect Point, used on another typical early 1900 souvenir plate exported from Austria. Made of porcelain.

Courtesy of Mrs. Ruth Charles.

The Niagara Falls Plate, green on white, manufactured by Buffalo China in New York State for their Historic Series of 1905-10. This is the only scene on their set of six ten-inch plates. All others featured well-known buildings throughout the U.S.

Courtesy of: Niagara County Historical Society, Inc., Lockport, N.Y.

Buffalo China also issued a smaller plate using the same art work as the larger one. The trademark on these plates was distinctive in that an eagle, rather than the firm's usual Buffalo, was used with the title of the scenes.

Although not originally made as souvenirs, the limited production of Carborundum Company Spode pieces from 1973 to 1976 makes them very collectible. This eight-inch plate was transfer printed and decorated in sepia or dark blue with 22 carat gold trim.

Courtesy of: Niagara County Historical Society, Inc., Lockport, N.Y.

2½-inch Solid Sterling paperweight. Reproduction of the placque over the Sir Adam Beck Generating Plant entrance, Canada.

Footed Victorian Jewelry Box. Cut glass with brass trim 3 x 2½ inches.

Hand painted German China pitcher. 11½ inches tall. C1900.

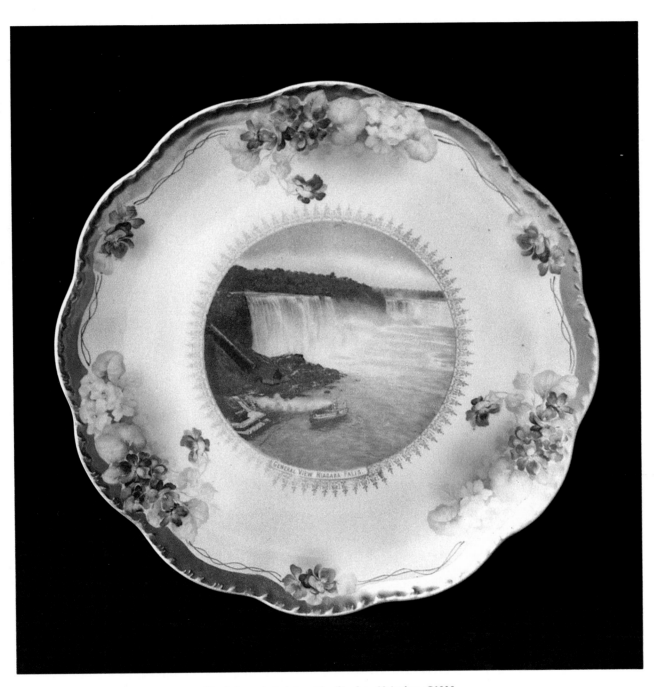

Hand decorated plate with gilt edge, 12 inches. C1925.

Bavarian Tea Biscuit Jar, 5½ inches tall. C 1900.

German made pitcher. 3¼ inches tall. C1925.

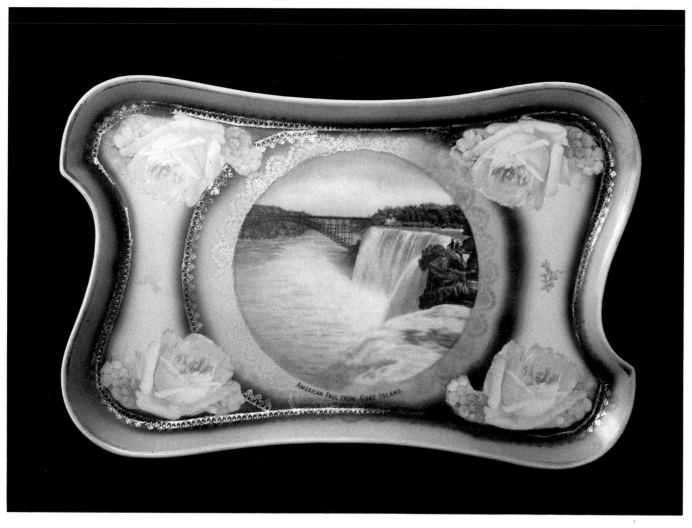

Vanity Tray, 11 x 7¼ inches. C1925.

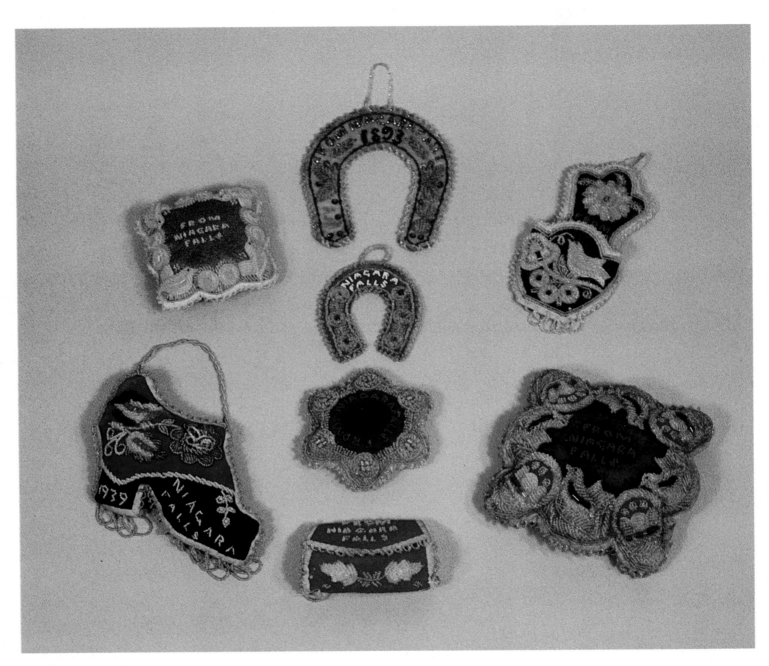

Indian Beaded Novelties, 1893-1939.

Typical selection of stock souvenir pieces of the Victorian Period, given regional interest by the application of Niagara Falls scenes. Made in Germany.

Courtesy of: The John Burtniak Collection, Niagara Falls, Ontario, Canada.

Pitchers were also selected from stock patterns such as these, for sale in local souvenir stores. Made in Germany, c 1925.

Courtesy of: The John Burtniak Collection, Niagara Falls, Ontario, Canada.

Mugs and drinking tumblers, 4½ inches tall, with scenes from Cave of the Winds, Prospect Point and Goat Island. Imported from Germany, c 1925.
Courtesy of: The John Burtniak Collection, Niagara Falls, Ontario, Canada.

Shaving mugs, popular souvenirs at the turn of the century and valued collectibles today.
The John Burtniak Collection, Niagara Falls, Ontario, Canada.

Although the Prospect Point scene is common, this 12-inch tall Austrian-made pitcher is a fine and rare piece. Hand painted decorations and gold trim accent it. c 1900.
Courtesy of: Mr. & Mrs. Norman MacAskill.

Hotel Ware: This rare find was purchased by a Niagara collector who recognized the words Cataract House. It is a water pitcher, part of a set that included a soap dish and wash basin.
Courtesy of: The John Burtniak Collection,
Niagara Falls, Ontario, Canada.

Wedgwood has always been popular for souvenir pieces. These picture the Honeymoon Bridge, dating them to c 1900.

Courtesy of: The John Burtniak Collection, Niagara Falls, Ontario, Canada.

Both the shape and scene are unique on this souvenir manufactured in Germany. The inclined tramway shown on the American side was destroyed by fire in 1892.
Courtesy of: The John Burtniak Collection,
Niagara Falls, Ontario, Canada.

Ruby flashed glass was mass produced at the turn of the century and localized by etching the name of the tourist area on pieces.
Courtesy of: Local History Dept., Niagara Falls, N.Y. Public Library.

Another popular souvenir of pressed pattern glass, ruby stained, with pinwheel design. c 1900.
Courtesy of: Mr. & Mrs. Norman MacAskill.

An inexpensive variety of china was also used for manufacturing souvenirs in the early 1900's. This milk colored plate, 7 inches in diameter, with cut work border, was made for threading a ribbon through to hang on a wall.
Courtesy of: Niagara County Historical Society, Inc., Lockport, N.Y.

Vases of milk glass, painted in orange, brown or green and trimmed with gold, were also popular souvenirs. These are German, c 1900.
Courtesy of: The John Burtniak Collection, Niagara Falls, Ontario, Canada.

Originally sold as The Niagara Falls Tray, this piece is of pressed glass with frosted scenic area. Sixteen inches wide, eleven and a half inches long, it is a rare and exquisite acquisition today. c 1885.

A fine Niagara Falls souvenir, probably from a jewelry store. It is beveled glass, a footed ring box, with brass trim. 3½ x 2 inches. c 1900.

Commemorative or limited editions of souvenirs are always exciting and historic finds. This one, made for a Shriners' convention in 1909, shows the Steel Arch Bridge and Cantilever Bridge above the Whirlpool Rapids.

Courtesy of: The John Burtniak Collection, Niagara Falls, Ontario, Canada.

Stock patterns in paperweights were ordered for souvenirs. Photos, taken from scenic postcards, were glued to the bottoms.

Courtesy of: The John Burtniak Collection, Niagara Falls, Ontario, Canada.

Paperweights: A large, heavy glass weight, 7½ by 3¾ inches, made for pens and pencils. Below, two others of stock or catalog choices available for souvenir shops.

Courtesy of: The John Burtniak Collection, Niagara Falls, Ontario, Canada.

Thick paperweights, distinctively shaped, were probably more expensive souvenirs. These are ¾ inch thick, dating to the early 1900's.

Courtesy of: The John Burtniak Collection, Niagara Falls, Ontario, Canada.

This unusual find demonstrates the popularity of Niagara Falls as a motif. It is an etched glass front door panel from a Victorian period home.

Courtesy of: Mr. & Mrs. Norman MacAskill.

These antiques fall into the precious category of Niagara Falls souvenirs. They are hand-painted Italian alabaster, made into Victorian period table ornaments. The bottom piece is taken apart to show the hand colored picture insert and piece of magnifying glass in top, through which to view the scene of the falls.

Courtesy of: Local History Dept., Niagara Falls, N.Y. Public Library.

CHAPTER 5

Niagara Silver Spoons

Souvenir spoons comprise the largest collecting category in silver. In fact, spoons were second only to china as Niagara souvenirs. Napkin rings, paperweights and finger rings of silver were not mass-produced as were spoons, and are far less common. They represent rarities for present-day Niagara Falls souvenirs collectors.

Just as transfer printing first made beautiful, decorative china affordable, so too, the development of machine cast and electroplated tableware brought ornate silverware to average households. Also, like china, spoon styles and patterns changed during the years that spanned the Victorian to pre-World War II periods. Since they were of American and Canadian make, there were gaps in production during World War I, the depression years of the 1930's, and again during World War II when metal alloys were diverted to defense needs. Souvenir spoons were manufactured on the east coasts of the United States and Canada.

Both Oneida and International Silver had factories in Niagara Falls, Canada, and produced quantities of spoons that were sold in the area. The Pan American Exposition, held in Buffalo in 1901, was featured on a series of souvenir spoons along with the falls. The Exposition drew the biggest crowds recorded, to that time, in Niagara history. It featured electric power transmitted from generators at the falls and the first display of electric lighting effects ever seen. This amazing spectacle, along with huge lights that illuminated the two falls, caused thousands of tourists to board excursion trains from Buffalo to Niagara Falls every half hour. Probably more souvenirs, particularly spoons, exited the area in the year 1901 than in any other given period of Niagara Falls history.

Niagara Falls spoons, as they are known today, were popular souvenirs of the 1901 Pan American Exposition because spoon collecting was a national fad at that time. The years 1890 - 1925 are known for this particular collecting craze. Spoons, like china, were made for such Victorian niceties as individual salt dips, demitasse coffee, morning or afternoon tea, cocoa, citrus fruit, and desserts. Lengths ranged from two to six inches. In addition to an array of souvenir spoons, including those that featured Niagara Falls, other novelty spoons were also being collected during this period; for example, baby spoon and fork sets, moustache and medicine spoons, and iced tea stirrers. Thousands of spoons were purchased in Niagara Falls souvenir shops and jewelry stores in the early 1900's. Most of them bore Niagara Falls designs, but others were made into souvenirs at jewelry shops where the words "Niagara Falls" were engraved in the bowls of selected fine-quality sterling spoons.

Prices were one to three dollars, plus 25 cents extra for gold-plated bowls! Today, these same spoons sell for $12, $15, and $20 each, determined by the sterling, silver plate, or gold plate content and any identifying manufacturer's marks that date them. The majority of the souvenir spoons were not marked because they were less expensive, promotional products manufactured by the prestigious silver companies for export to other than jewelry and department store outlets. In other words, the companies did not necessarily want their names on souvenir spoons. However, it was a period when newly discovered silver mines had made silver plentiful and cheap, forcing companies to compete for the popular market. It was also a time when all machine-produced items were new marvels eagerly sought by the buying public; the complete opposite of today, when hand-craftmanship is the rarity.

Spoons were made from flat, blank strips of a metal alloy consisting of copper, nickel and zinc. In one operation, the blanks were fed into two part die casting machines that simultaneously pressed both sides with an engraved or embossed appearing design and then stamped the blanks into spoon shapes. Although the spoons were mass-produced, very talented artist-designers transferred the designs from paper to handmade, hand-chased master models for use in making the dies (patterns) for the cutting and stamping machines.

After they were stamped out, rows of spoons, hanging from wire racks, were conveyed to electro-silver plating vats. Thickness of the silver plate was determined by the length of time during which the spoons were dipped. This plating was designated as standard, double, and triple, and spoons priced accordingly. The designations referred to the ounces of silver per gross of spoons and was often noted on the backs of spoons as: A, standard; AA, double; and AAA, triple. The word "sterling" was stamped on solid silver spoons, indicating that an industry-established standard had been met.

Although a great assortment of souvenir spoons were produced with Niagara Falls or Maid of the Mist motifs, several are worth describing because the details on them are known and also because they convey a slice of local history.

One, called the *Niagara Spoon*, was a special design patented for production by W. B. Durgin Co., Concord, N.H. The patent was held by W. H. Glenny, Sons & Company, of Buffalo. The spoon was sterling and featured the two falls and Goat Island on the stem with the word "Niagara" in relief down the side. It was available with a plain bowl or with a Whirlpool Rapids design in the bowl. The spoon sold in tea, coffee, orange and sugar sizes and prices ranged from $1.50 to $3.50. These spoons date to the 1896 - 1904 years.

Another stock souvenir spoon of the era, adapted as a Niagara spoon, is of interest because it featured the design known as *All America*, produced by the Sterling Co., Providence, R.I., between the years 1909 and 1929. The head of the handle shows a bust of an American Indian above a sheaf of corn, and the bowl has a scene of both falls from Prospect Point. A tomahawk, bow and arrow and two peace pipes decorate the reverse side of the handle. The spoons were made in tea and orange sizes, and there were relish forks to match. Indian heads were popular motifs on all souvenir spoons and particularly appropriate for Niagara Falls because of the Maid of the Mist legend and other regional Indian history.

Over the 90-year history of souvenir spoons, silver manufacturing companies merged, were bought out by larger companies, changed names, or ceased operations. All of this business activity helps spoon collectors identify acquisitions which have manufacturers' marks on them.

Oneida had manufacturing plants in both cities of Niagara Falls until 1914 when they closed the one in the United States. From 1925 until 1977, they maintained an elaborate showroom near the Canadian Falls, cleverly combining business and tourism. They still manufacture silver at Niagara Falls in Canada (but not souvenir spoons) and at their plant in Oneida, New York.

The International Silver Company, another competitor at the falls, became a huge conglomerate that swallowed up many smaller companies. Spoons marked International

Silver Company (ISC) date after 1928, because this company did not put its own name on silver before that year. Prior to that, the company retained the marks of the individual firms which it had taken over.

A thorough polishing of old spoons and a good magnifying glass will reveal the artistry and details of themes taken from Niagara Falls. The vertical shapes of the two falls adapted nicely to spoon handles and the circular rapids and rainbow fit well into spoon bowls.

Another fad followed that of spoon collecting. It was the bending of old spoons into rings and bracelets. Jewelry displayed for sale at antique shows or flea markets might easily include a Niagara Falls spoon that was adapted in such a manner during the 1960's and 70's.

Because they were used mainly for display, and compared to china and glass, were indestructible, Niagara Falls spoons are still in circulation today.

Silver spoons, turn of the 19th century designs, are of particular value today both for the silver content and historic details on them.
Courtesy of: Local History Dept., Niagara Falls, N.Y. Public Library.

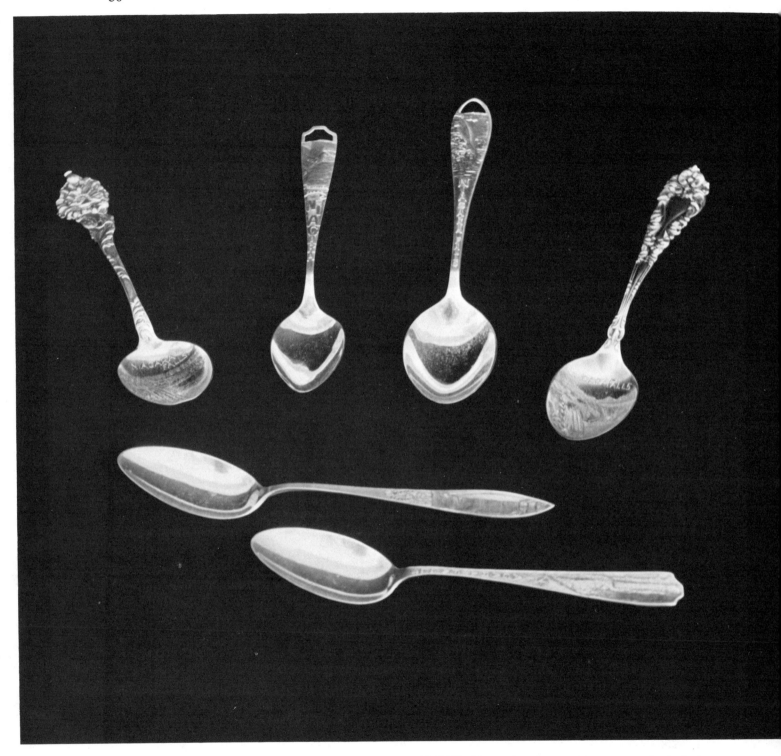

Silver spoons, mid 1900's, illustrating the transition to more simple designs.
Courtesy of: Mr. & Mrs. Norman MacAskill

Stock patterns in souvenir spoons made for display in spoon racks. The one on the right is the Niagara Spoon with personal initials added to the bowl.
Courtesy of: Mr. & Mrs. Norman MacAskill

Design closeups, L-R: Pan-American spoon with the Goddess of Light Tower and falls with a horse-shoe in the bowl; two of the Niagara Spoons manufactured for the W. H. Glenny Sons & Co., Buffalo, N.Y.; and an All-America fork.
Courtesy of: Local History Dept., Niagara Falls, N.Y. Public Library.

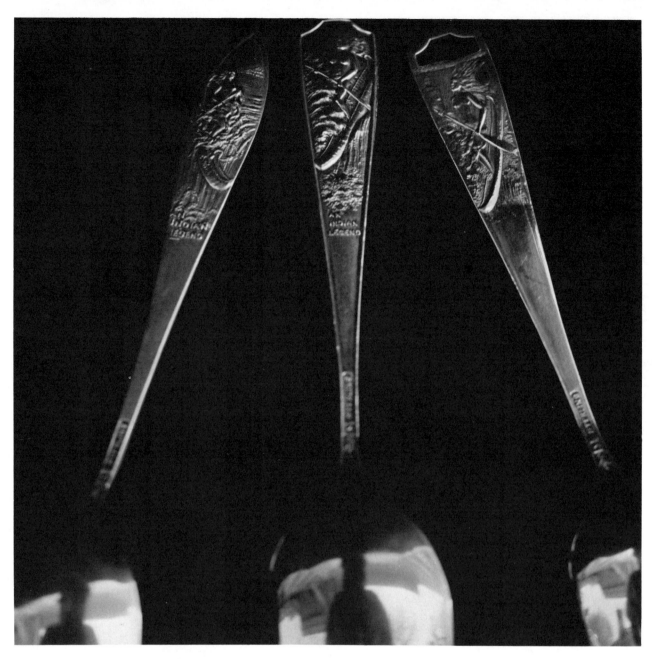

Souvenir spoon designs were stamped on both sides simultaneously in machine presses. These feature the Maid of the Mist legend on the reverse sides.

Courtesy of: Mr. & Mrs. Norman MacAskill.

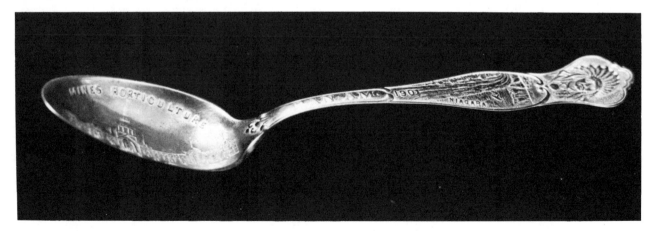

Pan-American Exposition souvenir spoon with the date, 1901, and falls motif on handle. Gold plated.

A rare and early Niagara Falls piece, this silver teapot warmer has white porcelain panels with lithopane designs of Niagara Falls. c 1860.

*This solid sterling paperweight is particularly valuable because it is a
reproduction of the plaque over the Sir Adam Beck Generating Plant
entrance on the Canadian Side. The scene is the Maid of the Mist's father
pursuing her canoe over the falls.*

Courtesy of: Mr. & Mrs. Norman MacAskill.

*Napkin ring, silver plated. Although many were manufactured, they do not
seem to surface for sale too often. c 1900.*

Courtesy of: Mr. & Mrs. Norman MacAskill.

CHAPTER 6

Novelties

Novelties present a study of miscellaneous, impulse item souvenirs. They run the gamut from beautiful one-of-a-kind Indian beadwork pieces and spar jewelry to mass-produced carnival merchandise that was called "gimcracks." This is an appealing category that reflects marketing trends and tourists' whims in buying souvenirs over the years.

Most novelties were stock selections made from salesmen's catalogs. The assortments were similar to today's novelty souvenirs; ashtrays, tape measures, darning eggs, stick pins, napkin rings, pill boxes, picture frames, fans, playing cards, photo novelties, and miniature "peep shows." They were intended to be merchandised as impulse items, selling for a single coin — a nickel, dime, quarter, or half-dollar — in an era when there was no sales tax to complicate transactions.

Today, many of those early "carni" souvenirs have taken on surprisingly high values because they were made of materials that no longer exist and involved some handworkmanship.

Each new product, whether cereal or an alloy, that resulted from electricity generated at the falls, was a wonder in its day, usually triggering a surge of popularity when used for manufacturing souvenirs. In earlier chapters, it was pointed out that Shredded Wheat became identified with tourism because of its modern factory, and that Oneida souvenir spoons were also products of the immediate area. At the 1901 Pan American Exposition in Buffalo, *The Goddess of Light*, a symbol that topped a 375-foot high tower, was powered by electricity from the falls and was highly featured on many souvenirs produced for that event. New alloys such as aluminum and tin, manufactured in the area, also attracted the fancy of tourists when made into souvenir items.

Beginning with a study of the earlier, circa 1900 handcrafted Indian beadwork and moving forward to mass-produced, pre-World II novelties, a student of social history can learn how souvenir selections changed over the years, as did lifestyles, tastes, and manufacturing technology.

Indian Beadwork

Like many of the Niagara Falls souvenirs-turned-collectibles, the most valuable pieces of Indian beadwork date back to that great Victorian/Edwardian Period of the 1890 - 1920 years. Indian women sold their beaded wares on street corners near the falls, at Queen Victoria Park in Canada, on Prospect Point, and Goat Island in the United States. Their merchandise included moccasins, toy birchbark canoes, beads, bracelets, feathered headbands, pipes, and necklaces, but only the souvenirs marked with the words "Niagara Falls" will be considered in this chapter.

Many of these pieces also bear a date. They were designed to meet the tastes and home styles of whites, not of Indians, and included pin cushions, needle cases, wall pockets, good luck horseshoes, purses, hearts, shoes, chickens and other decorative pieces for hanging on walls or for use as tabletop knickknacks. Beadworking was by no means a new craft for Indian women and girls.

The Indians of this area of North America were first introduced to glass trade beads in 1492 when Columbus thought he had arrived in the West Indies and named the Native Americans Indians. With the later arrival of Dutch, French, and English traders, as well as missionaries and colonists, glass beads became a common medium of exchange. They were manufactured in Venice, Czechoslovakia, Belgium, and England, mainly to meet the needs of fur traders in America and Canada. For example, in the early 1800's, one beaver pelt was traded for two pounds of glass beads at the Indian Trade Room in Fort Niagara. Beads changed hands many times, and Indians decorated their clothes profusely with them.

Missionaries taught Indian women to use needles and thread, replacing their traditional needles of bone and the use of animal sinew as thread. Sewing machines, introduced to the Indian reservations by 1866, increased both beadwork productivity and the variety of designs.

Most of the Niagara Falls souvenir beadwork pieces were created by Indians living on the Tuscarora Reservation near the falls. They were among the groups of New York State Indians then called the Iroquois Indians. Their crafts are now referred to as *Iroquoia*.

The process of making a piece of Indian beadwork required patience and skill. A paper pattern of the object was outlined on a piece of cloth. The top piece was usually cut from velvet in a dark shade of red, blue, or brown. The bottom was generally a glazed chintz fabric. Either a cardboard backing or pine needle stuffing was inserted before cotton tape was machine-sewn around the edges to hold the two pieces together. Designs drawn on brown paper bags were tacked to the velvet cloth with thread before the beads were painstakingly applied by hand. Although there were more than 200 colors of beads, most of the 1890 - 1930 pieces from Niagara Falls featured clear, rectangular tube beads of various lengths for embossing, with colored seed beads and white pony beads used for the finer details. The embossed or raised effect was created by placing more beads on a thread than space on the cloth allowed, so that the beads were looped or piled up. Indians favored colors from nature in their beadwork - green, blue, yellow, red, and brown. Early designs differ from modern ones in the sizes of glass beads used and in the embossed effects.

Today, Indians still make beaded items in contemporary designs, using tiny white and colored beads. Some are plastic, others are glass, imported from Japan. Their Niagara Falls wares are no longer sold on street corners, but at the Native American Center Turtle Building near the falls and at the Indian Village in Artpark, also near the falls.

Spar Jewelry

Niagara spar may well have been the earliest souvenir of Niagara Falls. Spar is gypsum, a white mineral. Enterprising hucksters gathered chunks, stones, and pebbles of spar from the Niagara riverbed and sold it to eager, unsuspecting tourists as petrified mist from the falls!

At the turn of the century, spar jewelry became a great fad. One concern, the Potters of Niagara Falls, New York, manufactured it for more than 60 years. The Potters had cut, buffed, and strung beautiful beads, chokers, lavaliers, and tiny barrels containing peephole scenes of the falls. Their pieces, though unmarked, are noted for details of design and fine workmanship and are considered valuable today. Since spar jewelry may be difficult to recognize, one usually has to ask for Potter items at antique outlets.

This jewelry, of so-called native stone, was not unique to Niagara Falls. Spar jewelry pieces were stock items in souvenir shops at other scenic tourist attractions throughout the country, much of it imported from England and Czechoslovakia. The styles of spar pieces, such as stickpins, pendants, or barrels, and a handmade appearance, may be clues to dating these souvenirs; but it is impossible to authenticate the origin of the spar from which they were made.

Mother-of-Pearl

Because they are becoming scarce, these 1900 pre-plastic era materials are very collectible today. Mother-of-pearl, the hard iridescent substance forming the inner layer of a mollusk shell, was used for inlaying various pieces such as jewelry, ornaments, buttons, and knife handles. Stock items, mostly of Japanese origin, were adapted as souvenirs of Niagara Falls by the use of decals applied to them by merchants. They were inexpensive, popular sellers at the time, not to be mistaken for quality mother-of-pearl. Strangely, even these gimcracks have increased in value in today's collectibles market because the same type of modern pieces are made of a plastic resembling mother-of-pearl, not the real item.

Bone and Ivory

Genuine, hand-carved bone or ivory pieces particularly interest collectors today. In contrast to mother-of-pearl souvenirs, these were originally more expensive gift selections. Letter openers, pens, and fans were among choices available in these materials. Many were made with tiny Niagara Falls scenes in them with built-in magnifying glasses for viewing. Obviously, ivory pieces are more valuable than those made of bone. Usually, the two can be distinguished from one another by appearance. Bone has a grain almost identical to that of wood, whereas ivory has no noticeable grain. The colors of bone and ivory are often similar, ranging from white to cream, although bone often tends to be whiter.

Today, these materials have been replaced by machine-produced plastic souvenirs, as in the case of mother-of-pearl. Older pieces of bone or ivory are particularly charming, not only for the materials and handworkmanship, but also because many of the items such as ink pens and ladies' accessory fans are no longer made or used.

Wood

Throughout the years, wood has been the most enduring material from which to make souvenirs, due not only to its beauty, durability, and variety of applications, but also to the fact that it was inexpensive and plentiful. For these reasons, wooden souvenirs have been easily available to a majority of buyers.

In the 1900's, woodworking was an easily taught skill used by large numbers of manufacturers. Many souvenirs from that period were made of pine, mahogany, walnut or maple. They were machine-cut, turned on lathes, and glued or nailed by hand. Brass hinges and locks were used on boxes. Stock pieces were converted to local souvenirs by the addition of photos or decals shellacked onto them at the factory. Many of these boxes came from England, Scotland, Czechoslovakia, and Japan before World War II. They pre-date the period of mass-produced wooden souvenirs. Names of the countries of origin, stamped on the bottoms of these souvenirs, add to historic value.

Today's wooden souvenirs, usually imported from Taiwan, India, the Philippines, and the Republic of China, are made of a modern source of inexpensive wood, Philippine mahogany, and with less fine workmanship.

Pre-Plastic Materials

As each wave of manufacturing crested, it brought to the public souvenirs representing that era's most reasonably priced raw materials. Tourists eagerly purchased such novelties. Today those materials, many of them obsolete, help date and add history to souvenirs that pre-date the mass-production era of our modern plastic society.

The most popular, and last, of the pre-World War II materials used for souvenirs are now of great significance to collectors. Aluminum, tin, celluloid, and bakelite — originally regarded as the materials from which those unworthy gimcracks were made — have now come of age.

Indian beaded novelties: Made on the nearby Tuscarora Reservation and sold by the Indians to tourists at the falls. These items were very popular sellers and are of particular interest today because each was a one-of-a-kind handmade piece.

Courtesy of: Nancy Engle.

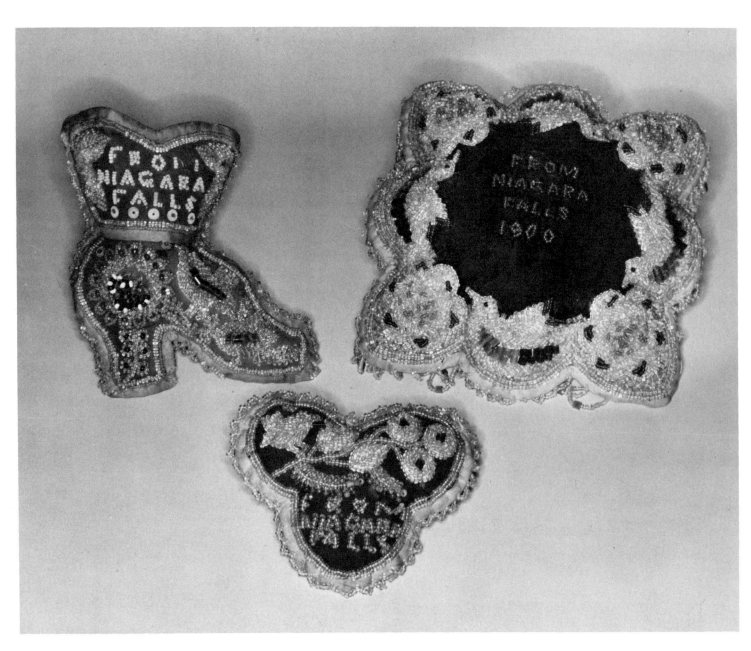

Indian beaded pieces made for Victorian homes.

Courtesy of: The Native American Center, Niagara Falls, N.Y.

Very early souvenirs, dating back to the late 1800's. These are window banners of linen and silk with hand painted scenes.

Courtesy of: Local History Dept., Niagara Falls, N.Y. Public Library.

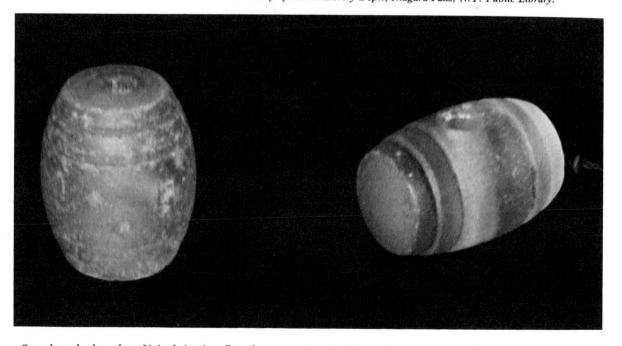

Spar barrels, less than ¾ inch in size. Popular souvenirs after Annie Taylor went over the falls in her barrel in 1901. Worn as lockets, each has a scene of the Horseshoe Falls inside.

Courtesy of: Local History Dept., Niagara Falls, N.Y. Public Library.

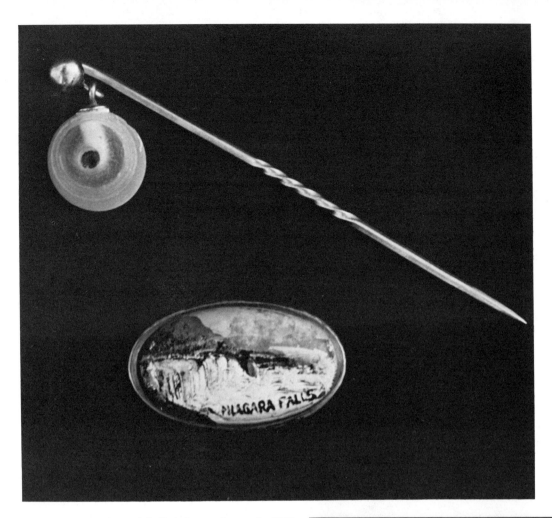

Spar stick pin and ladies dress pin, early 1900 souvenirs.
Courtesy of: Mr. & Mrs. Norman MacAskill.

Potter Family handmade jewelry of Niagara spar.
Courtesy of: Burton Rosenberg, Niagara Gift Shop,
Niagara Falls, N.Y.

Mother of Pearl calling card case containing a souvenir photo of the 1860 artist's rendering of the 'Maid of the Mist' boat trip through the Whirlpool Rapids.

Courtesy of: Charles Boyer

Bone ink pen with a magnified Niagara Falls view in the case.

Courtesy of: Charles Boyer

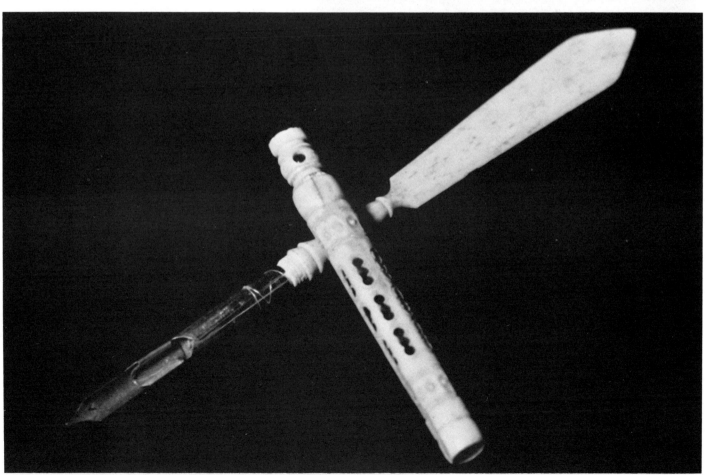

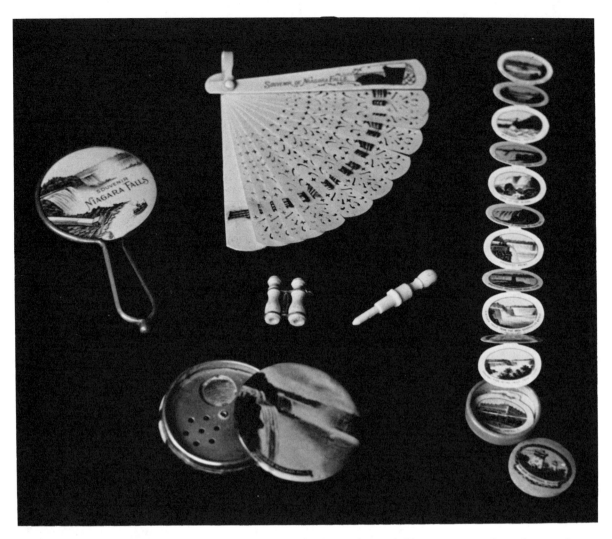

Novelty souvenirs such as these were small because they had to be carried in purses or pockets when tourists traveled by trains. Early 1900's.

Courtesy of: The John Burtniak Collection, Niagara Falls, Ontario, Canada.

Aluminum, fast selling when it was a new material on the market, was made into souvenirs. Shown are a drinking mug and dresser tray from early 1900's.

Courtesy of: Mr. & Mrs. Norman MacAskill.

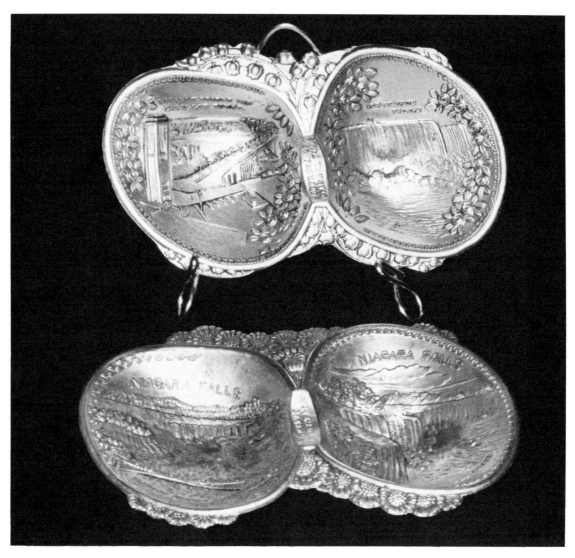

Pressed tin allowed more detailed scenes. These ash trays were made in Japan. The Carillon Tower, appearing in the upper left scene, pinpoints a date after 1948 when the Tower was built.
Courtesy of: Nancy Engle.

Baby rattle and pin box of wood, along with a ladies' dress pin, were among the early 1900 assortment of souvenirs marketed.

Courtesy of: Mr. & Mrs. Norman MacAskill.

Pressed wood scene on a jewelry box.

Courtesy of Nancy Engle.

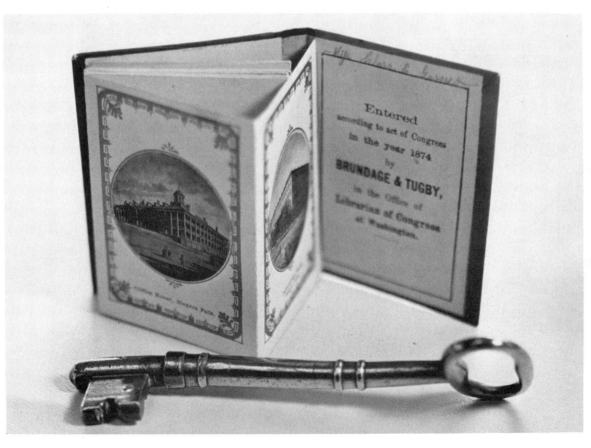

A novel combination: a souvenir booklet produced for the Tugby Store that once operated in Niagara Falls, New York, and the key to that store.

Buttons and badges are popular souvenirs from meetings held at Niagara Falls, which has long attracted conventions.
Courtesy of: The John Burtniak Collection, Niagara Falls, Ontario, Canada.

This collectible did not originate as a souvenir, but is now considered "crate art".
Courtesy of: Don Vidler.

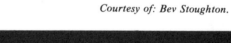

Miniature peep shows are typical of "carni merchandise" selections offered in souvenir shops. These are from the 1930's.

Courtesy of: Bev Stoughton.

Gimcracks from the "Roaring 20's" era.
Courtesy of: The John Burtniak Collection, Niagara Falls, Ontario, Canada.

CHAPTER 7

Paintings and Prints

Niagara Falls is regarded by art historians as the most universally painted scene on art works from the early to mid-1800's, years which represent a period of romantic landscape painting. Many great masters of the art world, as well as numbers of lesser and unknown artists, were lured to the falls by their breathtaking power and beauty. The volume of art work relating to the falls provides almost limitless material for study.

This chapter is an overview, concentrating only on scenes of the two falls and the history they reveal. The chapter concludes with an alphabetical listing of the more well-known artists whose works were reproduced as prints that were sold.

The first published, and perhaps the most long-lived souvenir of Niagara Falls, is the sketch done by Father Hennepin, the Roman Catholic Recollect Priest who was in LaSalle's 1678 expedition. He accompanied his sketch with a written description:

"Betwixt the Lakes Ontario and Erie, there
is a vast and prodigious cadence of water
which falls down after such a surprising and
astonishing manner, insomuch that the
Universe does not afford it parallel."

This sketch has been reproduced continuously in texts and was used as the basis for sketches by other early visitors who may not have done their original art work on the scene. Although Father Hennepin's 1678 sketch has endured the test of time because of its charm, it was not accurate. He was neither a cartographer nor a trained artist; therefore, his geography and perspective was incorrect.

The first true artists on the scene were later eighteenth and early nineteenth century military men - cartographers (map makers), officers, and soldier-artists who received formal art training at military academies in England. Their works were accurate, detailed records of the falls and surrounding geography as it then appeared, and are of great historic significance.

The early artists followed Indian trails through the wilderness from Fort Niagara to the falls and camped there for several days or weeks. There were no limits to the risks they were willing to take; clutching branches and bushes, they edged down the 165 foot banks to the base of the falls. There, they teetered on slippery rocks near Prospect Point, crawled on hands and knees behind the Luna Falls, and chanced canoe trips across to the Canadian side. Often, they had difficulty retracing their routes and lost their way. Like Hennepin, some artists kept written journals of their adventures, recording their feeling of overwhelming awe at first sight of the falls.

In those days, the drawing of vertical falls presented a new challenge. Artists were familiar with flat bodies of water such as lakes and oceans, but Niagara Falls demanded an amazing, new perspective. They pondered how to freeze, on canvas or paper, the constant play of colors on the clear water — colors ranging from the brilliant blue-reflected sky to aquamarine, to clear water over immense brown boulders. One of the unique features of the falls, for artists, has always been the clarity of the water. They also noted that they felt inadequate to convey the violent motion of the frothing, swirling rapids. Add to this the impact of the sound, and one can appreciate the reasons why those early artists felt overwhelmed. In a time when the atmosphere had not yet been penetrated by noises such as those emanating from factories, locomotives, or jets, and skyscrapers were beyond the mind's eye — the falls at Niagara must have provided an amazing audio-visual experience. Perfect rainbows that appeared (and still do) daily, were regarded not only as symbols of good luck, but also as rewards for the artists' strenuous efforts in getting to the falls before the area was developed for travel.

Following the military artists, many great masters of the mid-1800's visited the falls. The list includes Rembrandt Peale, John Trumbull, and John Vanderlyn, who were among the best known landscape painters from the famous Royal Academy in London. All three had studied under Benjamin West, the most renowned master of that era. Thomas Cole and Frederick Church, from the elite Hudson River School of landscape painters, created works that were also regarded as masterpieces. Another artist, best known for his Indian paintings, was also drawn to Niagara Falls. He was George Catlin. Primitive artist Edward Hicks, remembered for his "Peaceable Kingdom" paintings, also created a work of Niagara Falls art. August Kollner's sepia wash on line drawings are listed among the most outstanding works done of the falls.

The originals by these famous artists survive in public and exclusive private collections. However, there were prints and lithographs made from many of the originals, making possible ownership of this great art by the general public in the forms of engravings, aquatints, lithographs and chromolithographs.

Currier and Ives are the best known lithographers of the mid-1800's, but there were dozens of others in London, New York, Boston, and Philadelphia. Currier and Ives produced over 7,000 subjects of Americana, including five scenes of Niagara Falls. Their prints were done in sizes called folios: An 8½" by 11" sold for 15 to 20 cents; a 12" x 17" for 35 cents; and a 20" x 28" for $1.50 or $3.00 if handpainted. Today, these same prints sell for four to six hundred dollars.

Lithographers usually printed, in the picture margin, the name of the firm in the lower left corner, the title of the scene in the middle, and the artist's name in the lower right corner. A number in the border, for example 30/250, indicated that the print was number 30 in a run of 250. The lithographs (or prints) were tinted by an assembly line of women working at the publishing firm. Each woman hand-tinted one color on a print and passed it along to the next who added another color. Chromolithographs were a later development whereby color was added during the printing process.

Most American lithographs were not marked with a year and copyright words until after 1848. If a print is marked "entered according to the act of Congress" and the year, information about it is on record with the Register of Copyrights, Washington, D.C.

Photo offset, developed in the late 1800's, opened a new era in copying and distribution of art works. Today, this process is so sophisticated that it is difficult to distinguish a photo copy from an original unless one if familiar with the look and feel of old paper compared to new.

Following, in alphabetical order, is a reference to the better known artists whose Niagara Falls scenes were reproduced as prints. The list focuses only on scenes of the two falls, but it should be noted again that there was much art work done on the subject of the Niagara River.

1840   Bartlett, William H.: Prints engraved from his watercolor sketches are the best known and are still possible acquisitions for collectors. Bartlett was a talented and prolific artist who did many scenes in America and Canada. His Niagara Falls scenes were first published in 1840 in *Scenery of America, Volumes I and II*. He did six sketches of the falls that were made into engravings printed by George Virtue, London. Virtue Company also published Bartlett's prints in *Canadian Scenery*, an 1842 release that contained steel engravings taken from the original six.

1831   Bennett, William J.: Had his work published by H. I. Mergary, N.Y. He did four views of the falls.

1857   Church, Frederick E.: His 1857 oil painting of the Horseshoe Falls from near Table Rock is still ranked as the finest rendition ever done. Church was a prominent American landscape painter who specialized in natural phenomena. He was noted for his skill with color, light, rainbows and mist — all of which stand out in his world-famous 7 x 3½ foot canvas, titled, *Great Falls at Niagara*. It hangs in the Corcoran Gallery in Washington, D.C. Chromolithographs of the painting were printed by C. Risdon/Day & Son in England in 1857 and by Williams, Stevens, Williams & Co., of New York, after that year. Many copies in oil have been done, but none by Church himself. In 1868, Church did a second, vertical view from the American side that was also produced in chromolithographs.

1831   Cockburn, Lieut-Col. James Paterson: He was one of the military artists, stationed in Canada from 1826 to 1836. His watercolors were best known for the accuracy of details and perspective. His 1831 rendition, *Niagara Falls from the English Side*, was published as an aquatint by Ackerman & Co., London, in 1833. *View of Table Rock & Horseshoe Fall* was dedicated by the artist to Queen Victoria and made into aquatints by Ackerman in 1857. Cockburn did other falls area scenes that were also issued by Ackerman, a pioneer in the field of lithography.

1831   Cole, Thomas: Did his masterpiece, *A Distant View of the Falls*, that was reproduced in a number of publications including *Our Globe*, Malte-Brune's *History & Topography of the United States* and also engraved on steel by T. S. Woodcoch, Boston, and published by S. Walker in 1832. Cole returned to the falls in 1847 and did another scene titled *The Falls of Niagara*, that was reproduced by Louis L. Noble with other of the artist's works in an 1853 publication.

1760   Davies, Thomas: Another British officer stationed in Canada whose water colors and sketches are considered among the best for historical significance. His 1760 *View of the Great Cataract of Niagara* was engraved by J. Foregeron in 1760.

1807   Heriot, George: An artist, historian and Deputy Postmaster of British North America whose *Travels Through Canada* was published in London by Richard Phillips. The book included two views of the falls.

1751   Kalm, Peter: His descriptions of Niagara were published in *The Gentlemen's Magazine* in 1751, accompanied by a sketch based on Father Hennipen's original work. It was not done by Kalm, but assumed to have been selected by an engraver at the magazine publishing firm. *Facsimiles from Kalm, A.D. 1750,* was the title of engravings done by Ingraham's for this publication.

1849   Kollner, August: An artist and lithographer who worked with sepia wash on line drawings. His works are considered among the outstanding ones and were published in *Views of American Cities* in both color and black and white in 1849-51. *Rapids of Niagara, Done from Table Rock,* was one view published by Goupil, Vibert & Co., New York & Paris. Kollner also did *Terrapin Tower on the Brink of the Horseshoe Falls.*

1802   Vanderlyn, John: A highly respected landscape painter, and the first American artist to do the falls. Prints, titled, *A View from the Western Branch of the Falls, Taken from Table Rock, Looking up the River over the Rapids,* were engraved by F. C. Lewis and published in London in 1804.

1799   Weld, Isaac: A landscape painter from England who travelled in America in 1795-97. Views from his travels, including seven scenes of the falls, were published in *Weld's Travels* by I. Stockdale, Piccadilly in 1799 and went through several editions.

A View of the famous Cataract of Niagara, in North America.

One of many facsimiles of Father Hennepin's original sketch, done by those who did not get to see the falls for themselves when they wrote about it in the mid 1700's. This one, known as "Kalm's View", was engraved in 1751 and often reproduced in early texts and geographies.

Courtesy of: Local History Dept., Niagara Falls, N.Y. Public Library.

Titled: "View of the Horse Shoe Fall of Niagara" and published in Isaac Weld's Travels, *1795. This famous artist's works were frequently reproduced in texts and magazines.*

Courtesy of: Local History Dept., Niagara Falls, N.Y. Public Library.

"View of the Passage Under The Great Horse Shoe Fall": A lithograph from
a series of Niagara drawings done by A. Blouet, published in Paris in 1830.
Courtesy of: Local History Dept., Niagara Falls, N.Y. Public Library.

"The Schlosser Fall": *Also by Blouet, published in a series of lithographs in Paris, 1830. This scene depicts Prospect Point.*

Courtesy of: Local History Dept., Niagara Falls, N.Y. Public Library.

"The Falls of Niagara from above the English Ferry," a study done on the bank above the present Maid of the Mist *boat landing. It was produced by a military artist, Lt. Col. James Pattison Cockburn in 1833 and lithographed by Ackerman & Co., in London that year and again in 1857.*

Courtesy of: Local History Dept., Niagara Falls, N.Y. Public Library.

*Thomas Cole of the elite Hudson River School of landscape painters executed his famous paint-
ing in 1832. It was produced in steel engravings by T. S. Woodcock and published in Boston.*
Courtesy of: Local History Dept., Niagara Falls, N.Y. Public Library.

Bartlett Print titled, "Niagara From Near Clifton Hotel," was printed in Scenery of America,
published by N. P. Willis in London, 1840.
Courtesy of: Local History Dept., Niagara Falls, N.Y. Public Library.

Another of Bartlett's prints: "The Landing on The American Side below Prospect Point." 1840.

PLATE 7

AMERICAN FALL OF THE NIAGARA.

"American Fall of The Niagara": Reproduced in the late 1800's for a travel
book, offers a pleasing alternative to expensive original editions of prints.
Courtesy of: Charles Boyer.

*Niagara Falls, often was used as a backdrop for fashion illustrations. This
scene at Table Rock, made into an engraving, was printed in* Peterson's
Magazine *in the September, 1869, issue.*

Courtesy of: Niagara County Historical Society, Inc., Lockport, N.Y.

CHAPTER 8

The Stunters

In contrast to artists and poets who lingered at the falls to put down lasting impressions, the stunters (or daredevils) were tempted by the challenge of instant fame and fortune. Their antics lasted minutes, and few of them left with wealth. Some lost their lives.

There seem to be no parallels, no like characteristics, in the personalities or backgrounds of the men and women who decided to challenge the dangerous Niagara on ropes above the rapids or in barrels going through them. Aside from Blondin, an internationally famous tightrope walker of the late 1800's, the others were mainly inexperienced stunters of diverse backgrounds. For instance, one was a woman school teacher; another an Englishman, the father of eleven children. There were also a beautiful 23 year old girl from Italy, a chef from Buffalo, a Boston policeman, an airplane pilot, and a New York City Bowery barroom proprietor. They came to defy the falls and rapids, attracting crowds of thousands of people who lined the banks of both sides of the river to cheer them on. Those who survived to walk off their aerial ropes or climb out of home-designed barrels appeared more than slightly startled — admitting that they had greatly underestimated the Niagara River.

Stunting was a fad of the 1850 - 1900 era. At the same time that foolhardy people were taking on Niagara Falls, others of lesser ability or courage were doing stunts on smaller falls and rivers throughout the country. The idea had evolved with the circus movement in Europe and the novelty of flying trapeze artists. Aerial gymnasts became very popular. It follows that P. T. Barnum, the greatest promoter of the times, sponsored "The Great Blondin" of France for an appearance in America. What more spectacular place could he have chosen for a stunt than Niagara Falls? Blondin was to be the first to walk a rope from the American side to the Canadian side. No one believed he would succeed. Seating was built, bands played on both sides of the river, and thousands of people paid 25 cents each to line the banks of the American and Canadian sides on June 30th, 1859.

At 5:30 p.m. a starter cannon boomed and the public got its money's worth. Blondin held people spellbound in performances that were the first of their type. He was a showman to top all, with a keen sense of timing employed to build excitement. Deliberately, he hesitated and swayed on the rope as he edged from the American side toward the middle of the river. There, he stopped and lowered a line to the *Maid of the Mist* boat waiting below, drawing up a bottle of wine and casually drinking it before completing his walk. Just short of arriving at the Canadian bank, Blondin dumbfounded the already mesmerized crowd by doing a backwards somersault on the rope! After descending on the delirious crowds in Canada, he was given a champagne reception at which he announced his intention to return the same way he had come. He skipped and danced his way back across the river and into fame and wealth. For the remainder of the summer of 1859, and the next summer, Blondin performed regularly on his rope. Each show was a different routine. He crossed the rope on a bicycle, blindfolded, pushing a wheelbarrow, with his feet and hands manacled, and on stilts. Once, he pushed a small stove to the center of the rope, cooked an omelette on it, and lowered it to the passengers on the *Maid of the Mist* below.

Blondin also crossed the river carrying his manager on his back. Over 100,000 people watched them. The manager was terrified and they nearly fell as the rope swayed with their weight. The village of Niagara Falls, New York, awarded Blondin a medal for that performance. He was then 31. Returning to the Crystal Palace in England, his dangerous performances on the high wire continued to amaze audiences for years. Blondin died in his sleep at age 73.

The larger mementos of Blondin's Niagara Falls stunts — his bicycle, wheelbarrow, a length of his rope, starter cannon and cape — are in a museum in Niagara Falls, Ontario. A few poster ads for his performances and lithographs of his 1859 walk have survived the years as well as some stereographic views that were issued.

There were many successors to Blondin after that summer of 1859. Perhaps he made his stunts look so easy that they, too, thought they could gain instant wealth. Crowds came to cheer and jeer — but few ever surpassed Blondin's feats. Soon the idea of shooting the rapids occurred to those not agile on a rope. The first barrel stunt was done by a cooper from Philadelphia who designed his own barrel. Others came with their barrels, unaware of the force of the rapids, to try for instant fame. Two women shot the rapids in 1901. One made it, but the other died of suffocation. The first person to try going over the falls in a barrel was a woman, and she became the subject of a sad legend.

Mrs. Annie E. Taylor was a school teacher, 43 years old, from Bay City, Michigan. Her only objective in coming to Niagara Falls in 1901 was to take advantage of the crowds that would be available to watch her act in that year of the Pan American Exposition in Buffalo. She hoped to make a lot of money. She had designed her white oak barrel and hired an agent to promote her. Strapped in the barrel, padded with pillows, Mrs. Taylor lurched through the upper rapids toward the brink of the Horseshoe Falls. The overlooks were lined with spectators who gasped as Annie's barrel disappeared over the edge of the falls. Seventeen minutes later, when her barrel landed near the *Maid of the Mist* landing, Annie, dazed and bruised, was helped out of the barrel. She announced that, "Nobody ought ever do that again." Fame and fortune eluded her. The agent took the money and deserted her, and Annie, left alone, lacked the necessary showmanship to attract attention. She ended her days in the city of Niagara Falls, New York, sitting beside her barrel on Falls Street, selling autographed picture postcards of herself to passing tourists. It has been suggested that she also sold her barrel stays. Twenty years after her feat, penniless and blind, Annie Taylor died in a nearby poor house and was buried in a pauper's grave marked, "Annie Edson Taylor, First to go over the Horseshoe Falls and Live."

Others followed Annie Taylor's barrel act. Charles Stephens, the father of 11, lost his life; Jean Lussier of Quebec, designed a six-foot rubber ball of 32 inner tubes and survived to capitalize on selling small pieces of it for 50 cents each. George Stathakis, the chef from Buffalo, died in his 2,000 pound contraption when it got lodged behind the falls.

The stunt era lasted for more than 70 years, until World War II, when the Niagara River became off limits because of the nearby power plants. Today, stunting is outlawed, but once in a while an adventurer tries to boat through the rapids and has to be rescued. The challenge, not money, seems to be the greatest attraction. Certain types of personalities have steadfastly refused to believe that they cannot conquer the treacherous Niagara River rapids.

No period of Niagara Falls history drew bigger daily crowds to the falls than the stunt era. Souvenirs flowed into the shops and out with tourists who dispersed them throughout the world. Barrels became popular souvenirs in the form of salt and pepper sets, alabaster or Niagara spar stick pins and bracelet charms for ladies. Also, postcards, autographed photographs of the stunters, handbills and newspaper accounts of the performances were issued in quantities.

The stunters added spectacular human interest history to Niagara Falls and were responsible for the great tourist trade that brought money to area businesses, railroads, restaurants, hotels, and boarding houses — but little or nothing to those who took the risks.

W. J. KENDALL. Swam Niagara Whirlpool Rapids, Aug 22nd, 1886.
Copyrighted 1886, by J. T. BRUNDAGE.

Souvenir photos of two stunters. L-R: Capt. Webb, an English Channel swimmer, lost his life attempting to swim the rapids in 1833. William Kendall, a Boston policeman, was more fortunate. He succeeded in 1886.
Courtesy of: Local History Dept., Niagara Falls, N.Y. Public Library

Portraits of famous people were mass produced for sale in souvenir shops. This one is of Blondin, wearing the many medals and awards given to him for his famous stunts.
Courtesy of: Local History Dept., Niagara Falls, N.Y. Public Library

Annie Taylor being towed out for her barrel trip over the falls. October 24, 1901.
Courtesy of: Local History Dept., Niagara Falls, N.Y. Public Library.

"Noboby ought ever do that again," said Annie as she was helped from the river after her barrel trip over the falls.

Courtesy of: Local History Dept., Niagara Fall, N.Y. Public Library.

MRS. ANNA EDSON TAYLOR

Shot Horseshoe Falls (165 feet) October 24, 1901, and survived—a feat never before accomplished.

Entered barrel one and one-half miles above the Falls.

Was in barrel one hour and fifteen minutes. Had 32 pounds of air in barrel; 100 pounds weight on foot of barrel. Rescued six hundred yards below falls, on Canadian shore.

Poor Annie. She ended her days on a street corner near the falls selling picture postcards of herself standing next to her barrel. It is rumored that she also sold staves from her barrel as souvenirs, importing new ones when her own supply ran out.

Courtesy of: Local History Dept., Niagara Falls, N.Y. Public Library.

Stereoscopic views of stunters were sold in souvenir shops. Taken from original photographs, they are each accurate accounts of moments in history.

Courtesy of: Local History Dept., Niagara Falls, N.Y. Public Library.

Stunt activities were also produced on postcards.
Courtesy of: Local History Dept., Niagara Falls, N.Y. Public Library.

CHAPTER 9

Maid of the Mist

"Maid of the Mist" is the name of a legend and also of a boat line, both of which are featured on many Niagara Falls souvenirs.

The legend came first, dating back to an unknown origin, and is said to be a fantasy of white man's imagination. It is a lengthy legend, having to do with mysterious deaths of Indians in the Niagara area and the desecration of their graves.

In an effort to appease evil spirits believed to be causing the misfortunes, the Indians supposedly held a yearly ritual wherein they sent a beautiful maiden over the falls in a canoe filled with fruits and game. The sacrifice never succeeded until the chief's daughter was chosen to go over the falls. The legend continues that, after allowing his daughter to be sacrificed, the chief became remorseful and followed after her in his canoe, joining her in death. The result, legend says, was that the Maid of the Mist's spirit returned to her people to tell them to destroy an evil serpent in the river. The Indians succeeded in wounding the serpent, and it went over the falls and got caught in the rocks below. Supposedly, the dying contortions of the serpent shaped the Horseshoe Falls! The legend concludes that the serpent remains at the base of the Horseshoe Falls to this day, telling the gods that the Indians are protected.

Indian historians point out the fallacy of this legend in that Indians in this area of the country never offered human sacrifices to any gods or spirits. It was not a part of their culture. However, the Maid of the Mist legend prevails in poetry, art work and pageantry at the falls — including that of today's Indians — and adds a certain aura of mystery and enchantment that tourists enjoy.

Two paintings, *The Red Man's Fact* and *The White Man's Fancy*, were created about this legend and are seen on many souvenirs. *The Red Man's Fact* pictures the beautiful maiden in a canoe, going over the falls. *The White Man's Fancy* depicts a mythical figure of a Maiden with her arms upstretched, doomed to remain between life and death in the foam of the falls. They were created by James Francis Brown, a white artist, in 1891.

It was natural that the first boat operation to ferry tourists between Canada and the United States would attach the romantic name *"Maid of the Mist"* to its boat line.

Excerpts from an 1846 *Niagara Courier* newspaper describe the launching of the *Maid of the Mist I*:

"We regard the launching of this steamer as an event something more than ordinary. Taking everything into consideration, it is sublime reality. The scenery around the majesty of the thundering cataract above, the fierce rapids, the deep chasm through which dashes the river, the high embankments on both sides, the whirling waters just plunged from the fearful height, the ceaseless thunder of the great cataract bewildering the senses, the graceful gliding of "The Maid of the Mist" - combine to produce a sense surpassingly good and romantic. Whoever visits Niagara will not have seen half its wonder till they have taken a trip on the steamer *'The Maid'*."

That model, *Maid of the Mist I*, was a barge-like vessel built to carry a stagecoach and team of four horses. It was designed in the belief that there would be a stage route opened from New York City to Toronto and that Niagara Falls would play an important role in the route. The boat was a steamer, weighing 100 tons, with two smoke stacks. It is depicted on many paintings and souvenirs of that period, and is the only one of the series of the *Maid of the Mist* boats with two smoke stacks.

The ferrying business never materialized, but the owners soon realized that they could capitalize on sightseeing. In 1854, *Maid of the Mist II* was launched. It was a single stack, steam-driven boat with the distinguishing feature of a paddle wheel. There were more luxurious fittings on this boat and oilskin coats and caps to protect passengers who would be drenched on the exciting trip through the mist of the Horseshoe Falls. In 1860, the Prince of Wales (later King Edward VII) rode on the boat during his Niagara Falls tour, during which he also watched Blondin perform.

The following year, due to the impending Civil War and financial losses, *Maid of the Mist II* was sold at auction to a Montreal firm. One condition of the sale was that the boat had to be delivered to the Queenston dock in the lower Niagara River, which meant a trip through the Whirlpool Rapids, the Whirlpool, and the lower rapids. It had never been tried before. Although not advertised or intended as a stunt, this excursion turned out to be the most spectacular one ever undertaken. Enticed by a cash bonus, the *Maid's* captain, engineer, and fireman undertook the mission. Word of the event spread, and crowds appeared along the river banks. The boat headed toward the rapids, swirled out of sight, bobbed up minus its funnel and deck fittings, but survived the trip. The three-man crew emerged dazed and considerably aged. In fact, after that day, the Captain never again went near the river.

For the next 20 years, there was no *Maid of the Mist* boat operation at the falls. Row boats resumed carrying passengers back and forth between the Canadian and American landings. With the coming of railroads, there was an influx of thousands of tourists to the area, resulting in the launching of the *Maid of the Mist III* in 1885. The boat was superior to the previous models, able to go closer to the Horseshoe Falls. By 1892, business had increased so greatly that a sister ship was built to sail from a second landing on the American side. These boats did not cross from one country to the other. Cruises took tourists past the American Falls, Rock of Ages, beyond the Cave of the Winds, and close to the Horseshoe Falls before returning to the landings of origin.

Four *Maid of the Mist* boats have played a prominent part in much of the sensational history that has taken place around the falls. Today, as in 1846, to ride the *Maid of the Mist* is to experience Niagara Falls, and the Indian legend is still associated with the experience.

Greeting from **Niagara Falls, N. Y.**

The White Man's Fancy.

The Red Man's Fact.

The Maid of the Mist Legend was a natural one for which to name sightseeing ferry boats put into service in 1846.

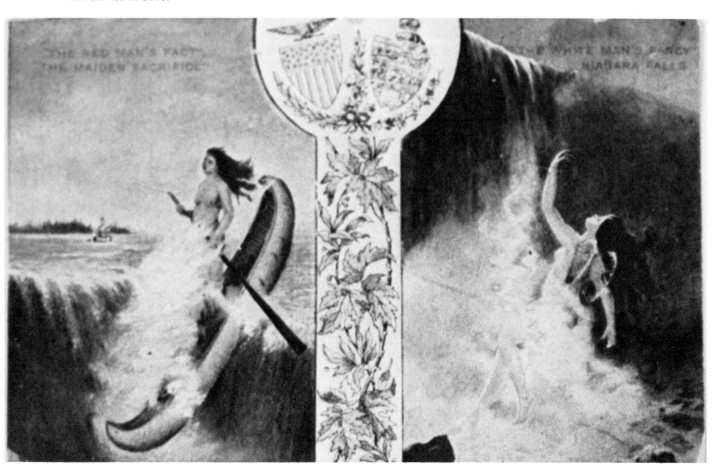

The legend was repeated for tourists on each boat trip to the Horseshoe Falls, resulting in souvenir postcards.

Courtesy of: Local History Dept., Niagara Falls, N.Y. Public Library.

Maid of the Mist postcards were, and are, favorites of tourists to the falls.
Courtesy of: Local History Dept., Niagara Falls, N.Y. Public Library.

In the late 1800's, trains brought crowds of tourists to the falls where they flocked to the Maid of the Mist *boats launched from docks on both the American and Canadian sides.*
Courtesy of: The Maid of the Mist Corp., Niagara Falls, N.Y.

Because of the crowds, enterprising promoters couldn't resist mocking up this replica of the second Maid of the Mist *boat and sending it through the Whirlpool Rapids (empty) as an advertisement in 1883.*
Courtesy of: Niagara County Historical Society, Inc., Lockport, N.Y.

In 1955, fire destroyed both Maid boats when they were in drydock being readied for the coming season.

Courtesy of: The Maid of the Mist Corp., Niagara Falls, N.Y.

Today, a fleet of four powerful Maid of the Mist *boats numbered I through IV continue to give tourists thrilling rides ever-closer to the thundering Horseshoe Falls. They are quite a contrast to the first steam powered* Maid of the Mist *launched in 1846.*

Courtesy of: The Maid of the Mist Corp., Niagara Falls, N.Y.

CHAPTER 10

Paper Treasures

This category includes picture postcards, leaflets, tourist guides, ticket stubs, menus, railroad schedules, and other printed descriptive materials. They are the throw-away, odds and ends, printed pieces that people tucked away years ago, just as we do today. The assortment of such good old bits of on-the-scene descriptive information is huge, particularly on the subject of Niagara Falls, because there was such an overwhelming quantity of material printed for publicity, promotion, and tourist business.

Paper treasures contain vignettes of past activities at the falls. They are found in attics, at flea markets, household sales, auctions, antique, and collectibles shows. Some are single, one-of-a-kind pieces. Others were carefully arranged in scrapbooks, photo albums, and diaries, or put away in plain envelopes. Most paper memorabilia is found in the forms of postcards, railroad materials, guidebooks, and brochures from attractions in the Niagara Falls area. Each of these topics warrants discussion, beginning with the most common impulse souvenir of all — the picture postcard.

Postcards

Postcards have always been the best-selling souvenirs. They pictured current on-the-scene views, and are therefore accurate records of past history. It is impossible to estimate how many picture postcards have been mailed from Niagara Falls in past decades. The Local History Department of the Niagara Falls, New York Public Library contains a collection of more than 7,000 postcards, each with a scene from Niagara Falls. This is just one repository. The volume of this collection indicates the availability of souvenir postcards. As a collecting category, today, postcards may be priced for resale according to the postage stamps on them, cancellation dates, pictures, or all three of these details. They bring from a nickel to four or five dollars, with common subjects such as "General View of the Falls" bringing the lowest price, and subjects of limited availability - the stunters, for example - getting top dollar. In this chapter, we are concerned only with the pictorial history found on old postcard scenes from Niagara Falls, not with postal stamps and cancellations.

Every special occasion, spectacle of nature, human activity, or new landmark resulted in photo postcard souvenirs: stunters, ice jams at the falls, *Maid of the Mist* boats, new bridges, restaurants, and so on. Often the postal cancellation dates pinpoint the years of such scenes, but lacking that, dates are often found in the sender's written message.

When Steam was King

In contrast to the prevalence of postcards, railroad memorabilia is not only scarce, but reflects a bygone era and one of the most exciting ones in Niagara Falls history.

In 1853, The Great Western Railway first rolled into Niagara Falls, Canada, ushering in a flamboyant, prosperous era of tourism that lasted for more than 50 years.

Locomotives, dubbed "iron horses", thundered into train stations on the American and Canadian sides of the falls, pulling passenger coaches which delivered thousands of tourists to the area each week. At the peak of the train traffic, prior to World War I, excursion trains arrived at the falls every half hour. Disembarking tourists were set upon by porters, horse and buggy coachmen, and vendors who waited at the stations to drum up business for hotels, sightseeing excursions, restaurants, and boarding houses in the area. No railroad bridge connected the two countries until 1855 when Roebling's famous Suspension Bridge, described in Chapter 3, was opened. Advertisements of the Great Western, New York Central, and Erie railroads claimed it to be "an attraction among the beauties and wonders of the locality." Papermobilia from this era may be titled, *The Great Railway Suspension Bridge* or *Suspension Bridge*. A collector who recognizes this bridge can acquire some valuable items.

During the train era, railroad companies competed fiercely with each other for the lion's share of passengers. Eventually, the big companies swallowed up the smaller operations. The Canadian National and New York Central railroads are most commonly associated with Niagara Falls, but there is papermobilia from other railways that once served the area. They were The Pennsylvania, Lehigh Valley and Michigan Central, each bringing passengers from various parts of the country. Other early lines transported tourists from the Erie Canal ports of Buffalo and Lockport to the falls. There was also a popular scenic train ride around the falls on what was known as "The Great Gorge Route."

Trollies, which were single, self-propelled passenger cars, were another kind of transportation powered by electricity from Niagara. They bridge the gap between the major train stations and the falls. For three cents, children could ride one of the big yellow trolley cars from Buffalo to Niagara Falls. During the Pan American Exposition, the International Traction Company trolley lines served the Exposition grounds in Buffalo, which they advertised as being: "within easy access to the marvels of the Niagara region." They carried thousands of passengers back and forth daily.

Like other peaks in Niagara Falls history, trains and trollies became outmoded with the advancement of technology, in this case, the coming of the automobile age. Trolley tracks are long gone, and much of the rural scenery that they once passed has vanished. But once a year, railroad buffs charter a train to make an excursion to "The Big Bridge" in an attempt to rekindle one of the great eras in this country's history, that of the railroads.

Guide Books

Guides to Niagara's wonders have been published continuously for over 150 years. These booklets offer accurate historic details on landmarks, bridges, scenic and tourist attractions; and the admission fees for specific years. The descriptive style of writing is the most charming thing about these items. For example, this excerpt from an 1885 guide book:

> "Many minds have essayed to reproduce Niagara literally, but the best attempts in poetry and painting have given only a very inadequate idea of its stupendous might, its everchanging play of color, its tremendous rush - its thundering roar. . ."

Such picturesque, adjective-laced writing reflects a pre-mass media era when the reading of the printed word was a leisurely pursuit. It offers an interesting contrast to concise present-day guides written for highly mobile tourists who may stop briefly at Niagara Falls en route from one airport to another.

The narrative style was very specific in early guide books, because they were used to conduct tourists verbally, book in hand, usually on foot, through the sights of the area.

> "Ascending the hill, turning to the right and advancing a few rods through the forest, you reach one of the most charming views of Niagara. . ."

Early guide books also warned tourists about hucksters and unwarranted fees and admonished them if they had not planned to spend sufficient time, at least a week, to do justice to the scenic wonder. Texts cautioned tourists not to slip "into the yawning chasm below" and did not hesitate to make editorial comments such as this 1892 reference to Terrapin Tower: "Its destruction was entirely unnecessary and took away a charming feature of Niagara."

All Niagara Falls guide books have contained material of a romantic nature. Glowing descriptions of the Bridal Veil Falls, the moonlight at night, rainbows in the late afternoon, and hand-holding newlyweds, enhanced Niagara Falls as *The Honeymoon Capital of the World*.

Early guide books, like the early souvenirs, were small, often measuring as little as 2 x 4 inches. Later ones, with hard covers and photo illustrations, measured 5 x 6 inches and larger. Dating them is usually no problem, because publication details were included along a border or in the front of books. Sometimes, a magnifying glass will be required to read such pertinent details.

Old guide books disclose the changing modes of transportation from rowboat rides across the river before the marvel of bridges, to horsedrawn surries and later excursion trains. Because the present tense was used in writing them, a reader can be transported back in time. It is a great experience to take one of these old guide books to the falls, follow its instructions, and sense the scenes as they appeared decades ago.

Postcards, the most common souvenirs of all, are a collecting category as well as accurate historical scenes from various periods of time. This assortment of folder scenes is from the early 1900's.
    Courtesy of: Local History Dept., Niagara Falls, N.Y. Public Library.

There were no regulations as to size or shapes of souvenir postcards in the 1920's when postage was a penny a card.

Courtesy of: Local History Dept., Niagara Falls, N.Y. Public Library.

In 1948, the United States issued a 3 cent stamp celebrating a century of friendship with Canada. It pictured the Railway Suspension Bridge designed and built by John Roebling.

Courtesy of: Local History Dept., Niagara Falls, N.Y. Public Library.

No. 205   STATE OF NEW YORK.   **Shares.**

NIAGARA FALLS BRANCH RAILROAD CO.

CAPITAL, $250.000.   SHARES, $100. Each.

This is to Certify, *That* _____ *is entitled to*

_____ *Shares of the Capital Stock of the*

NIAGARA FALLS BRANCH RAILROAD COMPANY,

transferable in person or by Attorney, on the surrender of this Certificate, at the

office of the Company.

Watertown, N. Y. _____ *18____*

_____ *Treasurer.*   _____ *President.*

Dividend seven per cent. per annum on this Certificate, payable semi-annually on the first day of May and the first day of November; guaranteed by the Rome, Watertown & Ogdensburgh Railroad Co.

Paper treasures include such items as this stock certificate issued in the late 1800's.
Courtesy of: Niagara County Historical Society, Inc., Lockport, N.Y.

Advertising slingers include descriptions and often prices relating to railroad service at the falls.
Courtesy of: Niagara County Historical Society, Inc., Lockport, N.Y.

"The Niagara Falls Route."

THE MICHIGAN CENTRAL

Parties contemplating a trip to Niagara Falls, St. Lawrence River points, the Adirondacks, the White Mountains, Boston and New England, or to New York and the seashore, will find full and valuable information as to rates, routes and connections in the new booklet issued by the Michigan Central, "The Niagara Falls Route," entitled "A Summer Note Book," which will be sent free to any address upon receipt of six cents in stamps to cover postage.

O. W. RUGGLES,
General Passenger and Ticket Agent,
CHICAGO, ILLS.

13

This unique piece is a label from Porter's Mills, dating to the mid-1850's.
Courtesy of: Niagara County Historical Society, Inc., Lockport, N.Y.

Timetable from the International Traction Company that operated from Buffalo to Niagara Falls. It contains specific details of history.
Courtesy of: Niagara County Historical Society, Inc., Lockport, N.Y.

Among paper treasures, nothing equals the descriptive prose in old guide books.

Courtesy of: Mr. & Mrs. Norman MacAskill.

Niagara Falls also inspired musical compositions.
Courtesy of: Mr. & Mrs. Norman MacAskill.

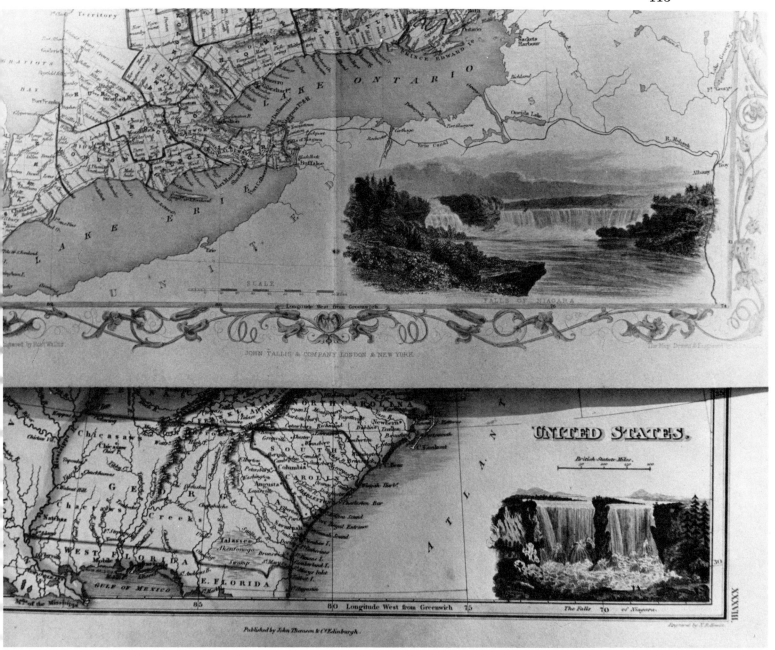

Old maps featured scenes from Niagara Falls.
Courtesy of: Mr. & Mrs. Norman MacAskill.

This advertisement mentions, "Fancy Goods Peculiar to Niagara" and suggests that visitors will do well to call at this place first.
Courtesy of: Niagara County Historical Society, Inc., Lockport, N.Y.

CHAPTER 11

Photo Memories

It is estimated that more film is, and always has been, exposed at Niagara Falls each day than at any other spot in the world. The illustrations in this book are a small testimony to the amount of photography that is available on the subject.

It doesn't matter who took them or who the people in the pictures are. What we can see are spontaneous records of tourists enjoying the falls. Snapshots are now regarded as a primary source in the chronicling of social history and folklore.

Although photo hobbyists have always prized historic pictures and cameras as well as the materials (i.e. glass plates, sheet film, etc.) on which pictures were once made; it is only in the last decade that the general public has found these items of interest and worth collecting and displaying.

Photographs of Niagara Falls include daguerreotypes, ambrotypes, tintypes, early paper prints, and cartes-de-visite, showing individual and group pictures and views of many now vanished landmarks and bridges. Each picture reveals two stories — an effort to freeze time, and the development of the art of photography as we know it today.

One of the earliest known tourist attractions at the falls, *Camera Obscura*, was the forerunner of photography. The Camera Obscura was first described in *Steele's Niagara Falls Guide Book* in 1834. It was a fascination to all tourists, and they willingly paid admission to what was simply a large, blackened room with a tiny hole in the wall facing the falls. Through the hole and with a lens and mirror arrangement inside, the falls scene was projected on the opposite wall or onto a tabletop. There were three camera obscura locations for fall's tourists. One was on the Canadian bank across from the American Falls, another was positioned to capture the Horseshoe Falls, and a third, at Table Rock.

The *Camera Obscura* was not a Niagara Falls related invention. Such devices date back to the days of Aristotle. In this country, artists traveled with tent camera obscuras in order to project scenic views for sketching. Later, the concept evolved as popular attractions at scenic area vacation spots. Camera obscuras were usually extolled in early guide books until the advent of photography at the mid 1800's. Collectors will recognize the names of the first kinds of photographs: ambrotypes, daguerreotypes, and tintypes. These were the forerunners of pictures made from negatives and printed on paper. They were very thin, fragile negative images, placed against a blackened background of metal, glass, tin, velvet, or paper. The effect was a picture, but it was usually reversed, unless the subject had been photographed through a mirror.

Early photographers worked with chemicals that were mixed on location and used immediately to coat a glass or metal plate. The plate then went into the camera wet. Each exposure might take up to 30 minutes, and the plate had to be processed immediately as it came out of the the camera. In those days, cameras were huge, supported by wooden tripods.

In looking at daguerreotypes, ambrotypes, and tintypes, it is sometimes difficult to distinguish one from another. Daguerreotypes were the first of the three, dating to 1839. They were invented by a French chemist, Louis Daguerre, who is credited with being the father of photography. One of the identifying (and annoying) characteristics of the daguerreotype is the tendency of the picture to disappear unless it is held in the correct position to a light source. These pictures were produced directly on highly polished, silvered copper plates, which gives them a second distinguishing characteristic — that of looking like silver on copper. Daguerreotypes tarnish in the same way that silverware tarnishes, but that doesn't mean that one should try to clean them with silver polish. Special chemicals and instructions are available from Kodak.

Ambrotypes, the second of the photographic processes, date from 1852 to 1875. They were underexposed negatives, backed with black paper or velvet, making them appear as positives. Again, the images were reversed. They were more reasonably priced than daguerreotypes because of the less expensive paper backing, and were quicker to make. They were very popular for portraits. Ambrotypes definitely look like thin negatives on dark backgrounds.

Tintypes, very sturdy little pictures, date from 1852 to as late as the early 1900's. They can be distinguished from the first two types of photo images by testing with a magnet. Tintypes will attract a magnet, the other two will not. The images were also reversed on tintypes. Many Niagara Falls group photos were made using the tintype method.

The invention of film and photographic papers advanced the production of photographs that were no longer reversed, and the affordability of them to the public. Stereo view cards viewed through stereoscopes, became a big hit.

The stereo cards were made by mounting pairs of identical flat photographs on cards and captioning them. Then seen through a stereoscope, a binocular-type device, a three-dimensional effect was created. In a time when there was no radio, television, or movies, and travel was still expensive and difficult, the stereograph was the television of its day, bringing scenes of America to every parlor. Black and white, brown-toned (sepia) and hand-tinted color stereo scenes conveyed America's scenic wonder, including Niagara Falls, to the homes of those not able to visit them in person.

Stereo cards, sold in souvenir shops, were mass-produced and very durable. Every facet of Niagara Falls history seems to have been recorded on them: bridges, stunters, railroads, ice jams, *Maid of the Mist* boats, and so forth. Many are available for collectors today at antique shows and flea markets. They offer the same enjoyment now that they did during the last half of the nineteenth century.

Cartes-de-viste (visiting cards) were also mass produced. Most of them were portraits, but there were scenic and architectural subjects as well. Cartes, as they are called by collectors, were mounted on stiff pieces of cardboard and often bear the date and subject's name. Imprinted matter on the reverse side is also interesting, giving details of the photographer's specialties, reorder prices, and sometimes his awards or exhibitions. Cartes are not rare, but offer some good collecting possibilities. Originally produced for 25 cents, they now sell for a dollar and up, depending on the rarity of the subject matter.

Roll film was the next invention in photography and the one that put cameras into the hands of tourists. The first camera was nothing more than a miniature concept of that big room, the *Camera Obscura*. George Eastman, of Rochester, New York, first marketed his Kodak No. 1 box camera in 1888, having created the name Kodak because it was easy to pronounce and spell. His camera sold for $25 and came loaded with enough film to take one hundred 2½ inch circular snapshots. It was necessary for the owner to send his camera back to Kodak for unloading, film developing and print making. Reloaded, it was then returned to the owner at a cost of $10. Early circular snapshots are very collectible and represent Eastman's inauguration of a new way of recording events — the common shapshot. Since that time, both the quality and quantity of professional and amateur photography of Niagara Falls has risen steeply.

There are many chances for locating early photographs, but a historian will look for the glass slides, 5 x 7 or 4 x 5 inches in size and old box camera negatives from which pictures were printed. These are original or source materials and more valuable than the pictures made from them. Every household sale and flea market seems to have boxes of negatives that people pass over. Hold them to the light and look for Niagara Falls subjects.

Light and heat ruin old negatives and photographs. Photographs should be printed from all negatives and copy negatives made of all photographs. The originals should then be given the same archival treatment and storage as paper. Custom enlargements can be obtained from the new sets of negatives. Tears, wrinkles, and missing corners that were on the originals can be corrected when new prints are made.

A Niagara Falls picture wall will allow enjoyment of the results of collecting photo memories, which, like the other souvenirs, convey the impressions and tastes of the constant parade of tourists visiting Niagara Falls.

Few collections offer the uniqueness of this one. As each wave of manufacturing and activity crested, it was brought to the public in the form of souvenirs made of that era's reasonably priced raw materials. Today, these materials, many of them obsolete, help date and add historic significance to the items.

Souvenirs of Niagara Falls continue to be created, making today's acquisitions tomorrow's history, while the subjects of all of this ongoing activity — the spectacular American and Canadian Horseshoe Falls — continue to attract and astound tourists.

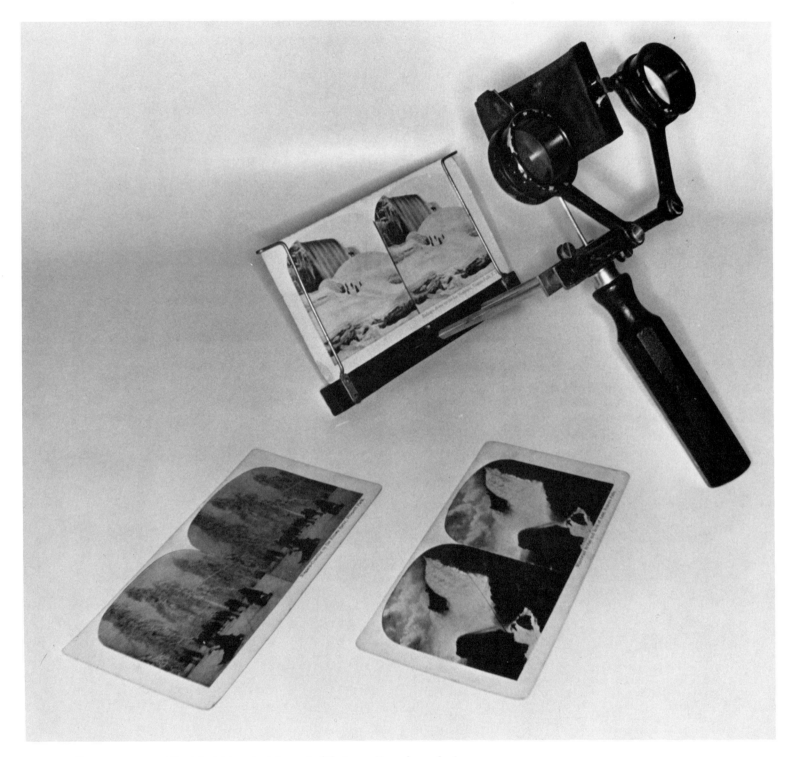

*Stereo scenes were the television entertainment of their era. Every home had
a viewer and selections of cards. Niagara Falls views were very popular and
sold in quantities at souvenir shops.*
Courtesy of: Aurora Historical Society, Inc., East Aurora, N.Y.

These stereo views of Terrapin Tower, a lost landmark, are valuable to both collectors and historians.

Courtesy of: Local History Dept., Niagara Falls, N.Y. Public Library.

Tintypes and ambrotypes offer slices of social history of people's visits to
Niagara Falls long ago.
Courtesy of: Local History Dept., Niagara Falls, N.Y. Public Library.

These are on-the-scene glass lantern slides taken and produced for sale by a San Francisco photographer before 1900.

Courtesy of: The John Burtniak Collection, Niagara Falls, Ontario, Canada.

In the early 1900's, 8 x 10 negatives were pressed between glass to make framed window pictures such as this one in a hand-hammered silver frame.

Courtesy of: Sue V. Rakow

Significant historic events, produced as souvenir photo packets, were
preserved forever by cameras.
      Courtesy of: Local History Dept., Niagara Falls, N.Y. Public Library.

Round snapshots were the first roll film pictures from the Eastman Kodak No. 1 Box Camera.

Personal photo albums are great sources for photo documentation of past events.

Courtesy of: The Maid of The Mist Boat Corp., Niagara Falls, N.Y.

Dramatic scenes from Niagara Falls were also produced for magazine and advertising purposes. This one is sepia colored, printed by The Detroit Photographic Co.

Pressure from the winter ice jam caused the Honeymoon Bridge to collapse in 1938. It was replaced by the present Rainbow Bridge.

Marilyn Monroe, snapped during the filming of the movie "Niagara". Produced at the falls in 1952.
      Courtesy of: The Maid of The Mist Boat Corp., Niagara Falls, N.Y.

More photographs were, and still are, taken at Niagara Falls than at any other place in the world.
Courtesy of: Local History Dept., Niagara Falls, N.Y. Public Library.

CHAPTER 12

Chronology of Scenes on Souvenirs

Biddle Stairs: On the U.S. side, near Cave of the Winds, 1829-1927.

Bridges: Cantilever (railroad bridge), built a few hundred feet up river from the
                       1855 Railway Suspension Bridge, 1883-1925.

                       Lower Bridges, located near the Whirlpool Rapids:

1st Suspension Bridge	1848-1855
Railway Suspension	1855-1897
Cantilever	1883-1925
Steel Arch	1898-1968
Whirlpool Rapids Bridge	1968 to present

                       Upper or Falls View Bridges:

Upper Suspension	1868-1898
Upper Steel Arch (also called Honeymoon Bridge)	1889-1938
Rainbow Bridge	1942 to present

Cataract House: On the U.S. side, 1815-1945.

Carillon Tower: Added to the Canadian end of the Rainbow Bridge in 1948.

Clifton House: On the Canadian side, original one built in 1833, burned down in 1895.
                       Second one, built in 1896, burned down in 1933.

Convent, The: Also known as The Loretto Academy. On the Canadian side. Appears
                       on the horizon line behind the Horseshoe Falls after 1880, the year it
                       was built. Burned in 1938. Rebuilt and still standing.

Hennipen's View: 1678

Horseshoe Tower: See Terrapin Tower.

International Hotel: U.S. side. Built in 1853, burned down in 1918.

Incline Railway: Canadian side, built to serve Maid of the Mist boat landing. 1894-1905.

Maid of The Mist
  Boat Numbers:

    I 1846-1854. Steam powered, two smoke stacks.

    II 1854-1860. Single stack, with a paddle wheel.

    III 1885

       1892 - duplicate model built to serve the U.S. side.

       1955 - both "Maids III" burned.

    IV Fleet of four now serving.

Prospect Tower: (see Terrapin Tower)

Railway Bridges: Suspension, Cantilever, Lower Arch.

Street's Pagoda: 1860, built above the falls on Cedar Island. Stood a short time. Appears infrequently in scenes.

Shredded Wheat Co: U.S. factory, 1901-1928.

Table Rock: Canadian side: First Rock slide, 1850. Removed by blasting, 1930.

Terrapin Tower: Also called Horseshoe Tower and Prospect Tower: 1833-1873.

CHAPTER 13

Pricing Guide

We all understand that antiques are generally worth what the buyer will pay! It is mostly a matter of time, place, desire and pocketbook.

One can only put a "rule of thumb" dollar value on the Niagara Falls Souvenirs pictured in this book. Even as the book goes to press, those values will already have changed.

We are talking mint condition. Items with cracks, chips or tears can be picked up for minimal amounts and are worth acquiring if the scene is rare or the piece very old. For the Niagara Collector, the scene may be his pleasure in a souvenir, not necessarily its condition.

Niagara Falls pieces are more expensive in their own backyard, Niagara Falls and Western New York. They are also more abundant there at household sales, antique shops and flea markets.

Staffordshire maintains its value over the years. Currently, a Niagara Falls serving platter can be priced as high as $500. Marked Wedgwood ranks in price with Staffordshire. Don't pay Wedgwood prices for Jasperware which can be an appealing alternative for under $100 per piece.

Ironstone, Spode, porcelain and bone china pieces are $50 to $200 depending on rarity. A 7½-inch Buffalo China Niagara Falls plate recently sold for $60. Common, smaller pieces that were mass produced from blanks and decorated with transfer prints have been purchased for 75 cents each at yard sales in Florida and for $5 and up at yard sales in the City of Niagara Falls, Canada.

Glass pieces, also mass produced from stock items for the souvenir market, are under $20 each. Paperweights are priced more by the size, shape and quality of glass then the scenes affixed to them. Niagara Falls paperweights range in price from $10 to $60. Those advertising extinct Niagara businesses seem to be more valuable.

Silver pieces fluctuate with the silver market. Sterling is rare. Silver-plated spoons that were mass produced and marked sell for $20 to $50 depending on the motif.

Among the earliest of novelty items are Indian beaded pieces. $50 can be a starting price for such one-of-a-kind items. Later novelty items, the "carni" or "gimcracks", offer a reasonable alternative to the more expensive Niagara Falls antiques. These little gems, along with buttons, badges and postcards, are sleepers to be found in boxes, bins and show cases. For $2 to $20, a Niagara Falls collector can have a rewarding treasure hunt in his travels.

Spar, bone, ivory, mother-of-pearl and wooden souvenirs range in price from $5 to $50. Not a very specific guide, but the collector must do his homework on these items.

Paintings and rare prints are a rich man's field. Original Niagara paintings by famous artists are up in the thousands of dollars. Prints and lithographs taken from those paintings are cheap at $1,000. Bartlett's Niagara Falls prints were seen for sale at $350 recently and a Currier & Ives for $700.

Posters, advertisements, handbills, slingers, guide books, postcards and a quantity of other printed items are also commanding a few dollars. Niagara Falls posters, depending on the subject and condition, have been for sale for as high as $75. Postcards start at 75 cents and may go as high as $5. Generally, for well under $100, a collector can acquire some good Niagara paper.

Railroad memorabilia and photographs include not only the Niagara Falls topic, but also collecting categories in themselves. The railroad buff or old photo collector will pay a good amount for flat pieces that a Niagara Falls collector might consider too expensive. It is impossible to specify prices on these items. Recently a collector paid $4.50 for a Niagara Belt-line time schedule and passed on a carte-de-visite for $11. Stereoptican cards begin at $5. And then there was a dusty old family photo album, containing the 1938 Honeymoon Bridge ice collapse scenes, for sale for $2.00!

Ultimately, the value of your Niagara Falls souvenirs will come from your knowledge of the subject as you go about collecting and from your ability to preserve and store the items properly so that they will increase in value while you are enjoying them.

Bibliography

Following is a selected list of further reading on Niagara Falls. Most of these books are available at local public libraries. Much more non-circulating material is available at the Niagara Falls, N.Y. Public Library, Local History Department and The Buffalo and Erie County Historical Society, Buffalo, N.Y.

Adams, E. D., *Niagara Power*, 2v. Niagara Falls Power Company, 1927.

Brong, Karl S., *Niagara Daredevils*, Star Printing, Newfane, N.Y., 1955.

Dow, Charles M., *Anthology & Bibliography of Niagara Falls, Vol. I & II*, State of New York, 1921.

Grabau, A. W., *Geology & Paleontology of Niagara Falls*, University of the State of New York, 1901.

Greenhill, Ralph & MaHoney, Thos., *Niagara*, University of Toronto Press, 1969.

Hulbert, Archer Butler, *History of The Niagara River*, Putmans, N.Y. 1908. Reprinted by Harbor Hill Books, Harrison, N.Y., 1978.

Kiwanis Club of Niagara Falls, Ont., *Niagara Falls, Canada*, Ryerson Press, Toronto, 1967.

Loker, Donald E., *Visitors Guide to Niagara Falls*, Stewart, Spiltalny & Son, Buffalo, N.Y., 1969.

Mason, Philip D., *Niagara and the Daredevils*, Niagara Daredevil Gallery, Canada, 1969.

Ritchie, William A., *The Archaeology of New York State*, N.Y.S. Museum of Natural History Press, 1965.

Vidler, Virginia, *American Indian Antiques of The Northeast*, A. S. Barnes, New Jersey & London, 1976.

Vinal, Theodora, *Niagara Portage from Past to Present*, Foster & Stewart Publishing, Buffalo, 1949.

Williams, Marjorie F., *A Brief History of Niagara Falls, New York*, Niagara Falls, N.Y. Public Library, 1972.

Index

Brackets indicate: chapter and paragraph locations of words indexed.